SpringerBriefs in Computer Science

Series Editors

Stan Zdonik
Shashi Shekhar
Jonathan Katz
Xindong Wu
Lakhmi C. Jain
David Padua
Xuemin Sherman Shen
Borko Furht
V.S. Subrahmanian
Martial Hebert
Katsushi Ikeuchi
Bruno Siciliano
Sushil Jajodia
Newton Lee

More information about this series at http://www.springer.com/series/10028

Channapragada Rama Seshagiri Rao
Munaga V.N.K. Prasad

Digital Watermarking Techniques in Curvelet and Ridgelet Domain

 Springer

Channapragada Rama Seshagiri Rao
Department of CSE
CMR Institute of Technology
Hyderabad, India

Munaga V.N.K. Prasad
Institute for Development and Research
  in Banking Technology
Hyderabad, India

ISSN 2191-5768   ISSN 2191-5776   (electronic)
SpringerBriefs in Computer Science
ISBN 978-3-319-32950-5   ISBN 978-3-319-32951-2   (eBook)
DOI 10.1007/978-3-319-32951-2

Library of Congress Control Number: 2016939431

Printed on acid-free paper

This Springer imprint is published by Springer Nature
The registered company is Springer International Publishing AG Switzerland

Abstract

A novel digital watermarking technique for color images using magic square and ridgelet transforms is designed, developed, tested, and described in this book. The novel feature of the method is to generate and use multiple copies of the digital watermark. This is tested for embedding digital watermark into color cover images and resulted in very high PSNR value and yielded comparable results with existing watermarking techniques. The book also deals with fractal coding technique for enhancing the robustness of the watermark techniques.

Six different techniques are designed, developed, and tested leading to the technique using magic square and ridgelets. Two other techniques are designed, developed, and tested using fractals. Chapter 1 discusses the fundamentals of digital watermarking like definitions, history, life cycle, properties, applications, classification, problems, and benchmarking.

Four digital watermarking techniques (image watermarking using curvelet transform (WCT), watermark wavelets in curvelets of cover image (WWCT), resized watermark into curvelets of cover image (RWCT), resized watermark wavelets into curvelets of cover image (RWWCT)) based on curvelet transform are discussed in Chap. 2. In WCT both the embedding and extraction procedures are discussed, where the watermark is embedded into the curvelets of the color cover image. In WWCT the wavelets of watermark are obtained. These wavelets are embedded into the color image curvelets. In the RWCT the watermark is resized based on magic square technique and then embedded into the color image curvelets. In RWWCT the resized watermark obtained through the magic square procedure is transformed through wavelet transformation and then the wavelets are embedded into the curvelets of the cover image. The results indicate that the embedding and extraction procedures of WWCT and RWWCT are much superior to WCT and RWCT. The regeneration of watermark image is satisfactory, but lossy.

Two more techniques (image watermarking based on magic square (MST) and image watermarking based on magic square and ridgelet transform (MSRTT)) are discussed in Chap. 3. In the MST the watermark image is resized through the magic square procedure and was embedded into the color cover image. In the MSRTT the resized watermark is transformed by ridgelet transformation. The color cover image is also transformed by the ridgelet transformation to obtain cells consisting of displacement and angle. The displacement values of watermark cells are added to cover image displacement values and the watermarked image is generated. The results indicate that the embedding and extraction procedures of MSRTT are superior to MST. The regeneration of watermark image is satisfactory, but lossy.

Two more techniques (digital image watermarking using fractals (DWF)) and digital image watermarking based on fractals and curvelets (DWFC) are discussed in Chap. 4. In DWF, the host image is encoded by the proposed fractal coding method. To embed the watermark evenly over the whole host image, specific range blocks are selected. Then, the scrambled watermark is inserted into the selected range blocks. Finally, the watermarked image is obtained by the fractal decoding method. In DWFC, the technique implements curvelet transform on the original color image to obtain curvelet coefficients. These coefficients are then transformed by using 2-level DWT to get LL2 and LL1 low-frequency sub-bands. The mutual similarities between LL1 and LL2 sub-bands are considered for embedding watermark. The obtained watermarked image has better quality when compared to a few exiting methods. The results indicate that the embedding procedures of DWF and DWFC are superior to MSRTT and extraction procedures of DWF and DWFC are comparable to MSRTT. The regeneration of watermark image is satisfactory.

Conclusions and future scope of work are discussed in Chap. 5. It is suggested that further work can be done in the following areas.

- The methods are tested only for compression attacks, so the techniques can be tested for various other image processing attacks like cropping, scaling, and rotation.
- The methods can be implemented and tested for video and audio watermarking.

Acknowledgement

"I've been blessed to find people who are smarter than I am, and they help me to execute the vision I have."—Russell Simmons

From the desk of Dr. C.R. Rao

Foremost, my heartfelt appreciation goes to my dearest wife Srilatha and to my daughter Chinmayi Sree Chitra for their motivation and support all the time in pursuing my research work.

I owe my deepest gratitude to my supervisor, mentor, and guide, Dr. Munaga V. N. K. Prasad for his continuous help and support in all stages of this book. I would also like to thank him for being an open person with ideas, and for encouraging and helping me to shape my interest and ideas. His unsurpassed knowledge has greatly helped me to grow from a student to a scholar.

I am deeply grateful to Dr. S. Ramamohana Rao, former principal of Geethanjali College of Engineering and Technology. His insightful comments and suggestions have been encouraging and supportive.

I would like to express my gratitude to Mr. Malla Reddy, chairman, and Mr. Gopal Reddy, Secretary, CMR Group of Institutions, and the other management members for their financial support. Their blessings and encouragement have always kept my spirits high.

I also thank Dr. M. Janga Reddy, principal, and all heads of the departments, CMR Institute of Technology, for providing enormous help to me. Generous support from my own department faculty, other staff members of the college, and friends has been encouraging.

I also thank Dr. Mantha Srinivas and Prof. D. Ramakrishna Rao from whom I have greatly benefited. Discussions with them have been illuminating and insightful.

Special thanks to the vice chancellor, and the director (R&D), Jawaharlal Nehru Technological University Hyderabad, and Mr. G. Ravinder Reddy, secretary, Teja Educational Society, for their support and encouragement. I would like to thank the head of the department and faculty, CSE department, JNTUH, for their encouragement in research work.

I owe my deepest gratitude to my parents for their invisible support and blessings.

From the desk of Dr. M.V.N.K. Prasad

My heartfelt appreciation goes to my wife Radha Devi, my daughter Jaitashree and to my parents for their motivation and support all the time. Special thanks to my Director, IDRBT, supervisor and to my colleagues.

Contents

List of Figures

List of Tables

Abbreviations

ASIC	Application specific integrated circuits
ATS	Adaptive Tabu search
AVC	Advanced video coding
BMP	Bit map file format
COCOA	Content and contrast aware
CRT	Chinese remainder theorem
DC	Discrete cosine
DCT	Discrete cosine transformation
DES	Data Encryption Standard
DHT	Discrete Hadamard transform
DSR	Dynamic stochastic resonance
DS-SS	Direct sequence spread spectrum
DWF	Digital image watermarking using fractals
DWFC	Digital image watermarking based on fractals and curvelets
DWT	Discrete wavelet transform
FH-SS	Frequency hopped spread spectrum
FHT	Fast Hadamard transform
FPGA	Field programmable gate array
FRAT	Finite Radon transform
FRWPT	Fractional wavelet packet transform
FWHT	Fast Walsh–Hadamard transform
GA	Genetic algorithm
GID	Group identification
GIF	Graphics interchange format
IF	Image fidelity
IFHT	Inverse fast Hadamard transform
IFWHT	Inverse fast Walsh–Hadamard transform
JPEG	Joint Photographic Experts Group
LFRs	Local feature regions
M-IGLS	Multicarrier/signature iterative generalized least-squares
MSE	Mean squared error

MSRTT	Magic square and ridgelet transform based technique
MST	Magic square technique
NC	Normalized correlation
NCC	Normalized cross-correlation
NMF	Nonnegative matrix factorization
NMSE	Normalized MSE
PCNN	Pulse coupled neural networks
PNG	Portable network graphics
PSNR	Peak signal to noise ratio
PSO	Particle swarm optimization
QIM	Quantization index modulation
QSVD	Quaternion SVD
RGB	Red green blue
RT	Ridgelet transform
RWCT	Resized WCT
RWWCT	Resized WWCT
SNR	Signal to noise ratio
SV	Singular value
SVD	Singular value decomposition
TAF	Tamper assessment function
Tiny GA	Tiny genetic algorithm
UID	User identification
VQ	Vector quantization
WCT	Watermark into curvelets of cover image technique
WWCT	Wavelets of WCT

Chapter 1
Introduction

Abstract Digital watermarking is a technique of embedding authentic information into digital content. It uses an algorithm for embedding watermarks to protect the copyright of digital content. It has become very important in various application areas like video, audio, text, image. Many authors have presented a number of watermark techniques. This chapter discusses the fundamentals of digital watermarking like definitions, history, life cycle, properties, applications, classification, problems, and benchmarking along with a number of techniques proposed by various researchers.

1.1 Introduction

The first digital camera was invented in the year 1975 by Steven Sasson, who was an electrical engineer at Eastman Kodak. The camera uses a charge-coupled device image sensor [1, 2]. This discovery led to the rise of digital image usage. The development of the Internet in 1990s has allowed the users to share the digital content across the globe. After 2000 the Internet availability has increased and it has become more simple and convenient for digital image sharing and accessing.

Electronic marketing (e-marketing) is a more popular marketing done with the help of the Internet technology nowadays, and it is one of the important application forms on the Internet. Wu Hongyu [5] presented an analysis about the role of Internet technology in promoting e-marketing and then discussed the advancement of e-marketing due to the latest technology in Internet technology. Carmona and Pelaes [3] presented the performance analysis of Voice over Internet Protocol and streaming videos in high definition through a residential indoor Power Line Communication (PLC) network, which allows data transmission at high speed by the power grid. Radio, N. et al. [4] presented an overview of the advancement of multimedia and real-time mobile applications, including the diversity of application types, their impact on the enterprise and consumer, their traffic volumes, and their load and communication patterns. They also discussed mobile video applications according to their communication characteristics and their distinct demands on the cellular network.

© The Author(s) 2016
C.R.S. Rao, M.V.N.K. Prasad, *Digital Watermarking Techniques
in Curvelet and Ridgelet Domain*, SpringerBriefs in Computer Science,
DOI 10.1007/978-3-319-32951-2_1

Multimedia devices like mobile phones, laptops make the information access easy. The online social networks, like Facebook, Hi5, are gaining popularity through information publication and sharing [6]. Piqing Xu et al.[7] discussed the importance of using multimedia in class to promote student's self-governing aptitude. Multimedia helps as a teaching technique for offering valuable teaching in current education. Multimedia gives a large amount of information to both teachers and students and strengthens their vision by improving teaching and learning efficiency. Chanmin Park et al. [8] discussed the concept of multimedia, the role of copyright, and the technologies that can be used to protect the copyrights of multimedia work. They have presented current issues on multimedia copyrights on the Web, and along with their suggestions to protect multimedia copyrights on the Internet. According to Royal Pingdom blog official news in 2012, the Facebook is adding seven petabytes of photos every month [2, 9]. The Internet gives extraordinary opportunities and benefits to its users with its huge networking. But in many cases the owners are concerned with the safety of digital content due to the possibility of producing imitations of their original content easily anywhere in the world. According to Havocscope Global Black Market Information News, Internet users have reproduced illegally more than 400 million digital files in the UK alone during Nov-2012 to Jan-2013 [10, 11]. Hence, advanced state-of-the-art techniques are required to arrest the forgery, unlawful sharing, and replication of information and rather normally used techniques to reserve the ownership rights, e.g., cryptography, steganography, digital signature, and watermarking [12].

Public key encryption transforms original files into another form. Without the decryption key the encrypted digital documents are not permitted to be viewed [12]. The sender has no way of monitoring how the receiver handles the information further after decryption. However, the digital watermarking technique does not change the originality of the cover image. The digital watermarks cannot be retrieved without suitable software. Further, sophisticated digital watermarks are being designed for the purpose of persistent in viewing, printing, or further distribution. Cox et al.[13] have given their literature survey stating that the watermarking and encryption techniques are different boats to sail to overcome the confusion about the buzzwords. Since 1990, a large group of researchers have shown their keen attention in Digital watermarking domain for its great potential in Internet world [12, 14].

1.2 Background

1.2.1 Paper Watermark

Paper was invented thousands of years before in China, whereas the term watermark has been derived from the German word "*Wasserzeichen*" [15, 16]. A watermark is defined as "A recognizable image or pattern in paper that appears as various shades of lightness/darkness when viewed by transmitted light (or when viewed by reflected light, atop a dark background), caused by thickness or density variations in the paper"

[17]. A traditional watermark on paper or currency is applied during production and remains an integral part of each paper or currency wherever it gets distributed [18, 19]. The paper watermark technique was discovered around 1282 in Italy [18]. In the eighteenth century, European and American paper industries started printing trademarks as watermarks on paper. The watermark can be applied to physical objects like fabrics, packing materials, and electronic signals.

1.2.2 *Digital Watermark: Definition*

A digital watermark is defined as "A kind of marker covertly embedded in a noise-tolerant signal such as audio or image data. It is typically used to identify ownership of the copyright of such signal" [20, 21, 23].

1.2.3 *Digital Watermarking*

Digital watermarking is "the process of hiding digital information in a carrier signal; the hidden information should, but does not need to contain a relation to the carrier signal" [20–22]. The digital signature embedded as a watermark should retain its integrity within the content, even after various manipulation attacks like compression, enhancement, cropping, embedding multiple watermarks, and filtering. The embedded signature can easily be extracted using suitable techniques. A watermark can be unique to one image or common to multiple images.

1.3 Digital Watermarking Process Life Cycle

A watermarking life cycle, shown in Fig. 1.1, is divided into three distinct steps: watermark insertion/embedding, image manipulation/attacks, and watermark extraction/detection [24, 25].

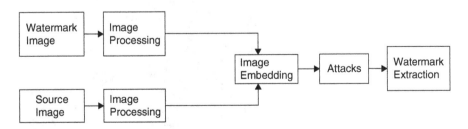

Fig. 1.1 Digital watermarking life cycle

1.3.1   Watermark Embedding

In watermark embedding a user can choose text information, like his contact details, a lucky number, as a watermark. The user can also choose an image, like a company logo, building images, or personal photos as watermarks, where these images can be gray scale images, black and white, or color images. These watermarks can be embedded in original or cover images with the help of embedding techniques. The output images are known as watermarked images. For example, Fig. 1.2 represents text information is considered for embedding into an image, Fig. 1.3. After embedding the watermarked image, Fig. 1.4 gets generated. These watermarked images can be communicated through the given communication channels.

1.3.2   Watermark Extraction

The owner of the watermarked image should prove the authenticity whenever the image gets duplicated without his consent. The author should retrieve the watermark from the watermarked image which has undergone the image processing

Fig. 1.2 Watermark   NAME

Fig. 1.3 Cover image

attacks through well defined extraction processing function. For example, Fig. 1.5 represents watermarked image meant for proving authentication. Figure 1.6 is the text information extracted from the watermarked image.

1.3.3   Watermark Attacks

When the watermarked images are shared or communicated through the communication channels, they get distorted because of various image processing algorithms like resampling, rescaling, compression, linear and nonlinear filtering, additive noise [26]. In these cases the watermarked images are expected to possess the watermark even after the attacks. Some of the attacks are removal attacks, geometrical attacks, cryptographic attacks, and protocol attacks [26, 27]. The watermark can be removed from the watermarked image by applying image processing techniques like denoising, lossy compression, quantization, demodulation, and collusion. The image processing attacks, like cropping, flip, rotation, shift, scaling, and translation, will destroy the existing watermark from the watermarked images. The cryptographic attacks try to embed misleading information into the watermarked images. Protocol attacks try to make those media meant for wide distribution unpopular.

Fig. 1.4 Watermarked image

Fig. 1.5 Watermarked
image

Fig. 1.6 Extracted
Watermark

1.4 Digital Watermarking Properties

A digital watermark possesses a number of properties. These are important to exhibit the proprietorship of the owner. Some of the properties are perceptual, fidelity, tamper resistance, modification and multiple watermarks, data payload, and computational cost [24].

The digital watermark embedded into the cover image is either perceptible or imperceptible depending on the technique applied. Most of the techniques embed the watermark imperceptibly so that breaking the authentication becomes complex. The watermark should be reliable to prove the authentication of the owner when it is extracted. It is very much important to ensure that the watermark does not lose its visibility threshold due to lossy compression attacks by the hacker. The watermark embedded should resist external attacks like image enhancement, color space manipulations, compression attacks, and should be perceptible for proving authentication. In some business software there is a need to insert a new watermark for every copy of the same to overcome the authentication problem. In some other cases it may be mandatory to insert multiple watermarks, so that to override each other watermarks to prove the authenticity. There is a need to minimize the data manipulation in the cover image so that it can be saved from heavy distortion due to embedding process. The computational cost is to be considered when a watermark to be embedded into data like image, audio, or video for commercial purpose. The cost will increase when it has to be inserted in multiple locations or when multiple watermarks get inserted.

1.5   Digital Watermarking Applications

Digital watermarking is a proven and existing technology that has been deployed in a broad range of applications like e-commerce, counterfeit deterrence, broadcast monitoring, forensics, rights management, copy prevention, content filtering and classification [24, 28].

1.6   Classification of Digital Watermarking Techniques

There are many watermark techniques in terms of their characteristics, application areas, and purposes. And they have different insertion and extraction methods [20, 24, 28] (Fig. 1.7).

Digital watermarking methods can be classified based on working domain, type of document, human perception, or application area.

1.6.1   Based on Working Domain

The watermarking techniques can be categorized into time and spatial domain and transform domain based on the algorithms applied. Enhancement of the input signal through filtering is the most acceptable processing approach in the time or space domain. A number of filter applications, like linear filter, causal filter, time-invariant

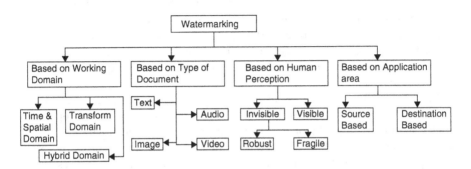

Fig. 1.7 Hierarchical representation of digital watermarking classification

filter, stable filter, and finite impulse response filter (FIR) are used under this process technique. A filter may also be described as a difference equation, a collection of zeroes and poles. The output of a linear digital filter for any given input may be calculated by convolving the input signal with the impulse response [24, 28].

To analyze the signal properties the frequency domain analysis is used. This allows studying the spectrum to determine which frequencies are present in the input signal and which are missing. The signals are converted from time or space domain to the frequency domain the transform techniques like Fourier transform (FT), discrete Fourier transform (DFT), fast Fourier transform (FFT), discrete Hadamard transform (DHT), Walsh–Hadamard transform (WHT), discrete cosine transform (DCT) [29, 30]. These transform techniques convert the signal information to a magnitude and phase component of each frequency. The transformation of signal is converted to the power spectrum, which is the magnitude of each frequency component squared. In addition to frequency information, phase information is also obtained. In some applications, how the phase varies with frequency can be a significant consideration. Filtering, particularly in non-real-time work can also be achieved by converting to the frequency domain, applying the filter and then converting back to the time domain. Frequency domain analysis is also called spectrum or spectral analysis.

1.6.1.1   Spatial Domain Techniques

The spatial domain techniques are defective against attacks as they manipulate pixel values directly. In recent years, many techniques were discussed using spread spectrum procedures [31, 32]. Hsu and Wu have stated that many techniques were discussed for embedding digital watermarks in mid frequency bands [33]. Sarwate and Pursley [34, 35] showed that the gold sequences for a given register length n there are more choices for the "key" than with shift m-sequences. Delaigle et al. discussed how to reduce the perceptual changes by using two level decomposition techniques [36]. Pickholtz et al.[37] defined spread spectrum communications as an approach of transmission, where the signal occupies excess bandwidth than required to transmit the data. The digital content is transmitted along with a secret code and is used at the receiver for reconstruction of the digital content. T. Kojima et al. have implemented a technique for converting secret text information like user identification (UID) and group identification (GID) by using CCC and to embed the same into the original image [35, 38–40]. It is also proven that the CCC technique is better than other spread spectrum sequence techniques based on m-sequences and gold sequences [41, 42].

E. Koch and J. Zhao [43] discussed a set of novel steganographic methods to secretly embed robust labels into image data for identifying the image copyright holder and original distributor in digital networked environment. The embedded label is undetectable, irremovable and unalterable. Furthermore it can survive processing which does not seriously reduce the quality of the image, such as lossy image compression, low pass filtering and image format conversions. Maxemchuk and S. Low [44] presented a technique for changing the amount of space between lines and characters of textual images for the bulk electronic publications, which was a major impact for electronic publishing to electronic publishing. Placing a unique, original recipient registered watermark in each copy reduces illegal redistribution so that the illegal reprints can be traced with the help of watermark.

Lin et al. proposed a method [45], to produce a robust watermark by using Gaussian distributions of pseudo-random numbers, with a zero average and unit variance, to resist the damages caused by Joint Photographic Experts Group (JPEG) compression. This way every block consists of dissimilar watermark, which is distributed evenly. The watermark in each block is regenerated by calculating the differences of adjacent pixels in spatial domain. Authenticity is verified by comparing the difference with a predefined threshold. The results of authentication through this technique are very acceptable, whereas the block size may affect its performance. Wu and Liu [46] presented a technique in which smoothness and successive degrees of block based image are calculated based on the priority of edge points, and then embedded the watermark in the high prioritized pixel locations.

Amnach Khawne et al. [47] presented a technique for image watermarking based on singular value decomposition (SVD) in L1-norm sub-space. The noise attack over watermarked image degrades its transparency and robustness. The L1 regression technique is used for calculating eigenvector. In this technique the elements of the left eigenvector applied for regression on each column of each block of attacked image and are estimated for L1 regression coefficients.

X.B. Wen et al. [48] presented an algorithm that takes the host image and divides the image into small blocks. For each block, a decision is taken for embedding watermark by verifying the possibility of using the block for embedding or not. This is mainly to avoid the perceptual degradation of the image. Trained probabilistic neural networks is applied to recover the watermark. Grace et al. [49] discussed semi-blind digital watermarking techniques using SVD. The techniques are robust and the watermark exists even after various signal processing manipulations. Chin-Chen Chang et al. [50] proposed a fragile watermarking scheme based on Magic Square Technique. In this algorithm a selected 3×3 magic square is embedded in every block of original image [2].

Wang Jing-pei et al. [51] discussed an SVD based watermarking technique. In this technique a meaningful text content is converted to hash sequence and then used as a watermark. This has solved the problem of protocol attack. Iman Omidvar Tehrani and Subariah Ibrahim [52] discussed a watermarking technique for protecting images from illegal redistribution. This method has chosen U component of SVD transformation for embedding the watermark. Karthigaikumar et al. [53] discussed a technique in which invisible watermarking processor with low power is implemented. The technique occupies less powered 457 slices. The technique is implemented both in field programmable gate array (FPGA) and Application Specific Integrated Circuits (ASIC). Mansorary et al. [54] discussed FPGA implementation techniques for fragile watermarking and to obtain 1112 slices at 350 MHz frequency in vertex 6 and 2103 slices at 260 MHz frequency in vertex 4. Jun Wang et al. [55] proposed watermarking method based on multi-objective genetic algorithm, which can automatically optimize system parameters, with a variable-length mechanism, which is designed to search the most suitable positions for embedding watermarks.

Reyes et al. [56] discussed an algorithm based on public video watermarking, where the strength of the watermark is proportional to the embedding energy. This robustness are limited due to degradation of video sequence caused by the same watermark signal. The security of the technique is increased by embedding a visually recognizable bit pattern like owner's logotype. Morteza et al. [57] discussed a technique based on SVD transformations. In this method the watermark image is transformed by SVD technique. Then the bits of the singular values are embedded to modify the specific bits of the singular values of the transformed host image. Most of the spatial domain watermarking techniques are not robust in nature, but simple for implementation. Chih-Chin Lai [58] discussed a watermarking method based on a tiny genetic algorithm (Tiny-GA) and SVD techniques. To consider the improvements of scaling factors the systematic approach of Tiny-GA is used. This helps to control the strength of the embedded watermark in this method. The watermark in the watermarked image exists even after various image manipulation attacks.

Rajlaxmi Chouhan et al. [59] discussed a technique based on dynamic stochastic resonance (DSR) and SVD procedures. The watermark is embedded by transforming the images using SVD transform technique. They have discussed a non-blind watermark extraction technique for extracting a grayscale watermark. Ray-Shine Run et al. [60] proposed a method based on SVD to protect the copyright of multimedia documents.

Dawen Xu et al. [2, 61] proposed a content based authentication watermarking scheme for H.264/AVC (Advanced Video Coding) video. Considering the new feature of H.264/AVC, the content-based authentication code for spatial tampering is firstly generated using the reliable features extracted from video frame blocks. The authentication code, which can detect malicious manipulations, but allow recompression, is embedded into the discrete cosine transform (DCT) coefficients in diagonal positions using a novel modulation method. Experimental results show that the proposed scheme can discriminate the malicious tampering from the mild signal processing. The tampered location can also be approximately determined according to the glide window and the predefined threshold. Karthigai et al. [2, 62] proposed a design to overcome the disadvantages like larger area and high power consumption. The algorithm used in it is prototyped in Virtex-6 FPGA. The results show that proposed design can operate at maximum frequency of 344 MHz in Vertex 6 FPGA by consuming only 1.1 % of available device. Zende and Chavan [63] presented a watermarking technique in which the encrypted watermark was embedded into zigzag locations of cover image pixels. Zigzag technique distributes the watermark across the cover image and does not allow tampering easily.

Boubiche et al. [64, 65] have presented a watermarking technique for robust data transfer in the networks. They have adopted two level security, where the first level is at higher layer and the other at the lowest layer of the protocol. Seed and Mohammad Ali Akhaee [66] have discussed a watermarking technique to overcome the tampering problem in the network. In this technique, they have manipulated least significant bits of every pixel by adding check bits and channel coded bits. These check bits are helpful in reconstructing a tamper proof image. Chandan Singh and Sukhjeet K. Ranades [24, 67] presented an image adaptive watermarking scheme for geometrically invariant and high-capacity data embedding scheme based on accurate and fast framework for the computation of Zernike moments (ZMs).

1.6.1.2 Transform Domain Techniques

A number of digital watermarking techniques were developed based on various transformation methods like Hadamard transform, cosine transform, and wavelet transform and other transformation functions [2].

1.6.1.2.1 Fast Walsh–Hadamard Transform (FWHT)

The advantage of Hadamard transforms in signal processing is its simpler implementation, low computation cost and high resiliency on low quality compression. The Hadamard transform [68, 69] array is defined as $H_n = H_n{}^* = H^T = H^{-1}$. Since H_n has N orthogonal rows $H_n H_n = N(I)$ (I is identity array) and $H_n H_n = N H_n H_n{}^{-1}$, thus $H^{-1} = H_n/N$. The inverse 2D-fast Hadamard transform (IFHT) is given as $[U] = H_n{}^{-1}[V]$ $H_n{}^* = H_n[V] H_n/N$. The Hadamard array of the order n is generated in terms of the Hadamard array of order n-1 using Kronecker product$\otimes$, as

$$H_n = H_{n-1} \otimes H_1$$

Or

$$H_n = \begin{bmatrix} H_{n-1} & H_{n-1} \\ H_{n-1} & -H_{n-1} \end{bmatrix}$$

The Hadamard transform [68] array is defined as
Forward:

$$H(u,v) = \frac{1}{N}\sum_{x=0}^{N-1}\sum_{y=0}^{N-1} f(x,y)\left[\prod_{i=0}^{n-1}(-1)^{(b_i(x)b_i(u)+b_i(y)b_i(v))}\right], \quad N = 2^n \quad (1.1)$$

Or

$$H(u,v) = \frac{1}{N}\sum_{x=0}^{N-1}\sum_{y=0}^{N-1} f(x,y)(-1)^{\sum_{i=0}^{n-1}(b_i(x)b_i(u)+b_i(y)b_i(v))} \quad (1.2)$$

Inverse:

$$f(x,y) \;=\; \frac{1}{N}\sum_{u=0}^{N-1}\sum_{v=0}^{N-1}H(u,v)\left[\prod_{i=0}^{n-1}(-1)^{b_i(x)b_i(u)+b_i(y)b_i(v)}\right] \tag{1.3}$$

The major disadvantage of Hadamard transform is not executing fast computations through modifications of FFT. Fast Hadamard transform is known as an extended version of the Hadamard transform and is defined based on recursive relationship property for transforming matrix, H, i.e.,

$$H_{2N} \;=\; \begin{bmatrix} H_N & H_N \\ H_N & -H_N \end{bmatrix} \tag{1.4}$$

Golub and Loan [68] used fast Hadamard transform (FHT) to propose an algorithm, which is one of the blind and symmetric digital watermarking techniques. Falkowski and Lim [70] used multiresolution Hadamard transform for embedding watermark. Gilani et al. [71] discussed multiresolution watermarking using Haar transform and Hadamard transform techniques. Ho et al. [72] proposed image-in-image water-marking method using Discrete Hadamard Transform (DHT). Li et al. [73] proposed block-based DHT method where watermark information is inserted into Hadamard coefficients using quantization for having improved watermark security. Maitya and Kundub [74] discussed data embedding based on information measure using DHT. Sarker and Khan [75] have discussed a blind watermarking technique based on Hadamard transform technique. In the given technique, the watermark was scrambled by using Arnold transform technique. The scrambled image and the cover images were transformed by using Hadamard transform technique and then embedded through embedding technique. The peak signal to noise ratio (PSNR) and normalized correlation (NC) obtained through this technique are 38.7 and 1 respectively. Chan et al. [76] have discussed a reversible fragile watermarking technique in Hadamard transform domain. In this they have embedded the given holo-gram into the Hadamard transformed host image.

1.6.1.2.2   Discrete Cosine Transform (DCT)

Lu et al. [77] discussed a method based on DCT. In this technique the original binary text is blurred for preprocessing and then secret information was embedded in the Discrete Cosine component of the original image. Dianwu Gao et al. [78] discussed an algorithm based on union chaos technology and the DCT theory which is a kind of technique based on the air zone image watermark algorithm. The results have indicated that the algorithm realizes watermark quite simply and the water-mark invisibility is good. The watermark process is having good resistance towards image cutting and JPEG compression. The algorithm's time complexity is low with good encryption effect and high security.

Roland Hu et al. [79] discussed a technique in DCT domain. The technique has measured the distortions to find the resistance capacity of each DCT coefficient based on the human visual system. Qiuping et al. [80] presented a method in the DCT domain. This method has considered the problem to identify the credibility of the paper archive. This method is applied to text and to other binary images.

Pengfei Wang and Yewang Chen [81] presented a watermarking process to be carried out during the JPEG quantization process. The process divides the images into small blocks of size 8×8 and then transformed by DCT. Based on the logistic system every DCT block is subdivided into four groups and all of the groups are check coded by the check bits to obtain the watermarked JPEG image. By checking the DCT groups the probability of tampering can be determined.

Reza Mortezaei and Mohsen Ebrahimi Moghaddam [82] presented a lossless watermarking technique based on fuzzy logic. Fuzzy integral is applied to find similarity between DCT coefficients of original image and watermark for watermark embedding. The experimental results have proven that the technique was efficient against various image processing attacks and the watermark extracted has visually similarities with the original one. Tsou and Li [83] discussed a method based on CCC technique. The CCC of watermark was produced by applying the technique given by Kojima [38]. Then the CCC is embedded into the DCT coefficients of the cover image.

1.6.1.2.3 Discrete Wavelet Transform (DWT)

A wavelet is a mathematical function which divides a continuous time signal into different scale components, where each scale component is assigned to a frequency range. A wavelet transform is the wavelet function representation [84]. The Fourier transform is considered to be a special case of prototype wavelet transform. But the only difference is that the Fourier transforms are localized in frequency where as the wavelets are localized in both frequency and time. The areas in which wavelet transforms can be applied include astronomy, nuclear engineering, signal and image processing, optics, fractals, radar, pure mathematics applications.

The Discrete Wavelet Transform function is defined as

$$\varphi_{(i,j)}(x) = 2^{-i/2} \varphi \left(2^{-i} x - j \right) \tag{1.5}$$

Where i, j represent the wavelet's width and position that scale and dilate the mother function.

Kundur and Hatzinakos [85] presented a method based on DWT. The technique can detect and localize any tampering with acceptable precision. It is robust against JPEG2000 compression that is based on DWT. Moreover, its security is based on the key security that must be transmitted separately through a secure channel. Inoue [86] invented a method that applies a DWT to the image, inserts the watermark in low frequency Sub bands and carries out an inverse DWT to obtain the watermarked image. This method allows the embedding of the watermark bits in the same block from which they were extracted, which help enabling good detection and localization of corrupted regions. The obtained watermark is then compared to the bits extracted for each block. If the number of different bits exceeds a predefined threshold, the corresponding block is considered altered. Otherwise the block is authentic. Joo et al. [87] presented a watermarking technique based on DWT for embedding watermarks into low frequency of the cover image. In this method, the cover image is transformed by using DWT. In case the coarsest level of decomposition is n, then LLn is selected and again 1-level DWT is applied on it. Chu et al.[88] discussed a method based on wavelets. In the given method, genetic algorithm was used to select appropriate zero trees in the wavelet transform, which helps to identify the quality and strength of the extracted watermark from the watermarked image after applying various attacks.

Hassanien et al. [89] used pulse coupled neural networks (PCNN) to enhance the contrast of the human iris image and adjust the intensity with the median filter. They used PCNN segmentation algorithm to identify the boundaries of the iris image and then used texture segmentation algorithm to isolate the iris from human eye. They then extracted texture feature from quad tree wavelet and then fuzzy C-means algorithm is applied to the quad tree for further processing of boundaries. The iris codes are extracted by using wavelet theory which then characterizes human iris. These codes are embedded into host images to identify the owner. In the authentication process, hamming distance metric that measure the recorded iris code and the extracted code from watermarked image is used to test whether the image is modified or not.

Huang Hui-fen [90] has suggested an algorithm for block scrambling of watermark images by using magic square technique and then embedding them in low frequency coefficients of discrete wavelet transform applied original image. Mohamed Ouhsain and Hamza [91] presented a technique based on discrete wavelet transform (DWT) and nonnegative matrix factorization (NMF). In this method the image is decomposed into four wavelet sub-bands and nonnegative matrix factorization (NMF) is applied to the blocks of each sub-band followed by an Eigen decomposition distortion step. The results have proven the robustness of the image watermarking scheme for copyright protection. Min-Jen Tsai [92] presented a visible watermarking technique based on the content and contrast aware (COCOA) technique with respect to the Human Visual System (HVS) model. The global and local characteristics of the host and watermark images in the DWT domain are utilized by the COCOA visible watermarking technique. For the best quality of perceptual translucence and noise reduction of the COCOA technique, the basis function amplitudes of DWT coefficients. Li Hui-fang et al. [93] presented a method in DWT domain. The method has decomposed the original and watermark images with DWT technique and then the DWT coefficient blocks of watermark are embedded to DWT coefficients of the original image blocks. The extraction procedure has proven the efficiency of the technique.

Feng Shi et al. [94] discussed a watermarking technique based on DWT. This has embedded the watermark in high frequency watermarks. The method has proven its inefficiency in dealing the image manipulation attacks like collusion attacks and cheating attacks. Gaurav Bhatnagar et al. [95] presented a digital watermarking technique based on fractional discrete wavelet transform technique for multiple image encryptions. The technique has encrypted various images by using a linear equation process and then applied embedding process. It has proven its efficiency of the embedding and extraction applications. Khalili and Asatryan [96] presented a watermarking technique in which watermark was applied to Arnold scrambling to obtain encrypted binary and was embedded into sub-images of the first channel wavelet decomposition of intended color space using block processing techniques. Tiwari et al.[97] discussed a watermarking technique based on DWT and Data Encryption Standard (DES) encryption techniques. In this method the encrypted watermark was embedded into the DWT transformed cover image coefficients. The results have shown that the method can withstand various attacks.

1.6.1.2.4   Ridgelet Transform (RT)

The ridgelet transform technique was introduced by Donoho in 1998 based on 1D wavelets [98, 99]. The wavelet transform is not suitable for producing the smoothness along edges and thus ridgelet transform was designed to have higher singularities.
   The continuous ridgelet transform (R) is defined as

$$R\left(a,b,\theta\right) \;=\; \left\langle \psi_{a,b,\theta}, f \right\rangle \tag{1.6}$$

$$\psi_{a,b,\theta}\left(x\right) \;=\; a^{-1/2}\psi\left(a^{-1}\left(x_1\cos\left(\theta\right) + x_2\sin\left(\theta\right) - b\right)\right) \tag{1.7}$$

Where Ψ represents mother wavelet.
   Patrizio Campisi et al. [100] discussed a watermarking method based on Ridgelet Transform technique. In this, they have identified the edges of the watermark image and then segmented to small blocks on which ridgelet transform technique was applied and then embedded into the original image. Yuancheng Li [101] discussed a method to embed the watermark by first transforming watermark image by Arnold scrambling method, and then embedding into the lower frequency sub band in the ridgelet transform domain.

1.6.1.2.5   Curvelet Transform (CT)

In 2000, Candes and Donoho introduced the curvelet transformation techniques, which is based on ridgelet analysis of radon transform of images [98]. The curvelets are special forms of wavelets, which is becoming a popular technique for multiscale object representation in image processing. When an image consisting of smooth curves is zoomed, the edges appear to be straight. Curvelet is defined based on this property and uses higher resolution curvelets for curves having bounded curvatures [98, 102]. However, photographs will not possess this property.
   Changjiang Zhang and Min Hu [103] discussed a watermarking technique based on curve let transform technique. In this, the watermark was first scrambled by the Arnold transformation. Then the watermark is embedded to the coarse coefficients, which are larger than some threshold values in the curve let transform domain.

1.6.2 Based on Type of Document

The watermarking techniques can also be classified based on the content on which watermark is applied, i.e., watermark embedded into Text, Image, Audio or Video. Users are replicating the text information designed and developed by others by downloading through the internet by causing copyright problems. To overcome this type of problem, text can be inserted into documents along with certain types of watermarking like number of spaces between words, page justification, pre formatted text style [24, 28]. The digital photos are more vulnerable to hackers who penetrate into one's memory to copy and publish their photos to create the copyright problem. To overcome such type of the problem there is a need to protect the images through various watermarking techniques. Digital audio published on the internet usually gets distributed by many net users. In 1954, Hembrooke filed a patent describing a method for the identification of music signals through the embedding of inaudible codes, with the objective of proving ownership, which can be considered as the time of the invention of digital watermarking [104]. The watermarking can be applied to protect the illegal distribution of audio files. Any video is a combination of bunch of continuous images and background audio effects. So watermark can be inserted either in images or in audio or in both. Due to the size of video files, the scope of embedding watermarks is much higher and also the chances of distracting the same are quite less. It also allows to hide the authentication information easily.

1.6.3 Based on Human Perception

The watermarks can be categorized to visible and invisible watermarks. Visible and invisible watermarks serve to prevent theft. Visible watermarks are useful for transmitting an immediate claim of ownership. The visible watermarks are perceptible to the human eye such as company logos and television channel logos. These watermarks can be extracted easily without any mathematical calculation and also can be destroyed easily. The invisible watermarks are not perceptible. And the type of watermark and the position of the watermark embedded are secret. Hence, only the authorized people can extract the watermark through some mathematical calculations. This kind of watermarking is more secure and robust than visible watermarks. Fragile watermarks, which get destroyed with slightest modifications, are used in integrity proof. Semi-fragile watermarks, which resist the slightest transformation, but get disturbed, are used to detect evil transformations. Robust watermarks are those which allows the author to prove their identity even after unacceptable transformations and are used in copyright applications and copy protection applications [24, 28].

1.6.4 Based on Application Areas

The application areas generally play a major role in classifying the watermarking techniques. According to application the watermarking techniques can be classified as source based and destination based watermarking techniques. The source based watermarks help to identify or authenticate ownership in a simple method. In this author identification gets embedded in the original image and its copies get circulated. In the destination based watermarking each distributed copy gets a unique watermark identifying the respective buyer. This helps the seller to trace the illegal reselling [24, 28].

1.7 Contemporary Problems in Digital Watermarking

The watermarking technology has to overcome many disadvantages. Some of them are related to originality of the image, noise, and retrieval of the watermark. The watermarked image should appear as if the original image after embedding a watermark, i.e., the qualitative perception of the watermarked image should be comparable to the original or cover image even after watermark gets embedded. All the signals transmitted through air or any other communication channel generally gets affected by electrical interference and implies noise over the signal. Due to such noise over the communication channel the embedded watermark should not be destroyed and moreover it should be recoverable. The extraction procedures must be well defined such that they overcome the noise problem and also not complicated. These should allow the users to authenticate themselves with efficient watermark retrieval [105, 106].

1.8 Benchmarking in Digital Watermarking and Performance Evaluation

Benchmarking is the process of verifying the obtained results, effectiveness by comparing with already existing results merits and demerits. The benchmarking improves the quality of the development activity. Some of the digital watermark benchmark tools, like StirMark and JEWELS, are available online. The performance of the digital watermark can be calculated based on various parameters and variables connected with embedding and extraction processes. The parameters and variable depend on the digital watermarking systems like private, semi private and public and asymmetric watermarking systems. A few parameters are based on amount of embedded information, watermark embedding strength, size and nature of the picture, secret information. The robustness of the digital watermark technique depend on the Human visual system, which is often neglected. The performance of the digital watermarking can be calculated with the help of pixel based metrics, perceptual quality metrics, structure based metric. The evaluation process should test a number of images with the changing nature for calculating the performance of the technique [26].

1.8.1 Pixel Based Metrics

The digital images possess their differences in their pixel values. Hence a number of different distortion metrics were defined to find the difference between original and distorted images and these are not based on the human visibility system. Some of them are mean square error (MSE), normalized mean square error (NMSE), signal to noise ratio (SNR), peak signal to noise ratio (PSNR), image fidelity (IF), normalized cross-correlation (NCC). This metric is having weakness related to brightness and contrast, visibility of low-contrast differences [26].

1.8.1.1 Mean Square Error (MSE)

This measures the average of the squares of the errors between any two images. When the MSE is low the quality of the image will be better [107].

$$MSE = \frac{1}{mn} \sum_{i=0}^{m-1} \sum_{j=0}^{n-1} \left[I_{i,j} - K_{i,j} \right]^2 \tag{1.8}$$

Where m, n represent the number of rows and columns, I and K are pixel values of originality and attacked watermarked images, respectively.

1.8.1.2 Peak Signal to Noise Ratio (PSNR)

It is defined as the ratio between the maximum possible power of a signal and the power of corrupting noise that affects the fidelity of its representation. The PSNR must be larger to have the best quality of image [107, 108].

$$PSNR = 10 \cdot \log_{10} \left(\frac{MAX^2}{MSE} \right) \tag{1.9}$$

Where MAX is the maximum value of a pixel in the matrix. MSE stands for Mean Square Error.

1.8.2   Perceptual Quality Metrics

This metric measure the quality of the images based on human visual system related parameters like luminance adaptation, contrast sensitivity, visual masking, and Visual channels. Some of the metrics examples are the visible differences predictor (VDP) and visual discrimination model (VDM) [26].

1.8.3   Structure Based Metrics

This metric detect structural changes in the image. The structural similarity index metric (SSIM) is one metric related to this principle [26].

1.9   Constitutions of Digital Rights Management

The Berne Convention, an international agreement governing copyright, was first accepted by all Berne union member countries in Berne, Switzerland, in 1886 and modified at Paris in 1971 [109]. The countries have realized the importance of intellectual property rights (IPR) after the establishment of the World Trade Organization (WTO) in 1995. The copyright is supposed to occupy the front position in economical development among the rest of IPRs. Digital rights management (DRM) is a term generally referring to protecting the copyrights of digital media files. The protection of the digital images can be enforced through encryption and decryption, steganographic or digital watermarking [110–113].

1.10   Summary

The chapter includes a brief introduction to digital watermarking, history, digital watermarking life cycle, properties of watermarking, attacks on watermarked images, digital watermarking applications, classifications of digital watermarking, contemporary problems of watermarking, benchmarking, and performance evaluation procedures for watermarking techniques. It also discusses the constitution of digital rights management (DRM).

References

1. David Prakel, "The Visual Dictionary of Photography", Lausanne: AVA Publishing, 2010.
2. Rama Seshagiri Rao Channapragada, Anil Srimanth Mantha & Munaga V. N. K. Prasad, "Study of Contemporary Digital watermarking Techniques", International Journal of Computer Science Issues, Vol. 9, Issue. 6, 2012, No. 1, pp. 456-464.
3. Carmona, J.V.C & Pelaes, E.G., "Analysis and Performance of Traffic of Voice and Video in Network Indoor PLC", IEEE Transactions of Latin America, Vol. 10, Issue. 1, 2012, pp. 1268-1273
4. Radio, N., Ying Zhang & Tatipamula, M.; Madisetti, V.K., "Next-Generation Applications on Cellular Networks: Trends, Challenges, and Solutions", Proceedings of the IEEE, Vol. 100, Issue. 4, 2012, pp. 841-854.
5. Wu Hongyu, "A Study of the Linkage Development of Internet Technology and E-Marketing", Third International Conference on Intelligent System Design and Engineering Applications (ISDEA), 2013, pp. 187 – 189.
6. Younggue Bae & Hongchul Lee, "A Sentiment Analysis of Audiences on Twitter: Who Is the Positive or Negative Audience of Popular Twitterers?", 5th International Conference on Convergence and Hybrid Information Technology, 2011, pp. 732-739.
7. Piqing Xu, Lingjun Zhao & Jiajun Liu, "Effective learning based on multimedia in college education", International Conference on Computer Science and Service System (CSSS), 2011, pp. 2209-2211
8. Chanmin Park, Seunghyun Kim & Taehyung Wang, "Multimedia Copyright Protection on the Web - Issues and Suggestions", IEEE International Symposium on Multimedia (ISM), 2012, pp. 274-277.
9. URL: http://royal.pingdom.com/2013/01/16/internet-2012-in-numbers/
10. URL: http://www.havocscope.com/tag/music-piracy/
11. URL: http://www.guardian.co.uk/music/2009/jan/17/music-piracy
12. Tsz, Kin Tsui, Zhang, Xiao-Ping P, "Color Image Watermarking Using Multidimensional Fourier Transforms", IEEE Transactions on Information Forensics and Security, Vol. 3, No. 1, 2008, pp. 16-28.
13. Cox I.J., Doerr G.,& Furon T., "Watermarking is not cryptography", Proc. Int. Workshop on Digital Watermarking, 2006, pp. 1–15.
14. Adil Haouzia & Rita Noumeir, "Methods for image authentication: a survey", Multimedia Tools Applications, Vol. 39, 2008, pp. 1-46,
15. D. Hunter, "Handmade Paper and its Watermarks: A Bibliography", New York, NY: B. Franklin, 1967
16. Divecha, N.; Jani, N.N., "Implementation and performance analysis of DCT-DWT-SVD based watermarking algorithms for color images", International Conference on Intelligent Systems and Signal Processing (ISSP),2013, pp. 204-208.
17. Biermann, Christopher J. "Handbook of Pulping and Papermaking (2 ed.)", 1996, San Diego, CA: Academic Press.
18. Meggs, Philip B. "A History of Graphic Design", John Wiley & Sons, Inc. publications, Third ed., 1998.
19. D. Hunter, "Handmade Paper and its Watermarks: A Bibliography", New York, NY: B. Franklin, 1967.
20. Ingemar J. Cox. "Digital watermarking and steganography". Burlington, MA: Morgan Kaufmann, 2008
21. Nicolo Zingales, "Digital Copyright, 'Fair Access' and The Problem of Misuse", Boston College Intellectual Property & Technology Forum, 2012
22. I.J. Cox, M.L. Miller, J.A. Bloom, "Digital Watermarking", New York, NY: Academic Press, 2002.
23. K.-C. Liu, "Colour image watermarking for tamper proofing and pattern-based recovery", IET Image Processing, Vol. 6, Issue. 5, 2012, pp. 445–454

24. Chandan Singh, Sukhjeet K. Ranade, "Image adaptive and high-capacity watermarking system using accurate Zernike moments", IET Image Processing, Vol. 8, Issue. 7,2014, pp. 373–382.

25. Boato, G., Conci, N., Conotter, V., De Natale, F.G.B. & Fontanari, C., "Multimedia asymmetric watermarking and encryption", Electronics Letters, Vol. 44, Issue. 9, 2008, pp. 601-602.

26. M. Kutter and F.A.P. Petitcolas, "A fair Benchmark for image Watermarking Systems", Security and Watermarking of Multimedia Contents, Proceedings of SPIE, Vol. 3657, 1999, pp. 1-14.

27. N. Hayashi, M. Kuribayashi, & M. Morii, "Collusion resistant finger printing scheme based on the CDMA-technique", International Workshop on Security, 2007, pp. 28–43.

28. Christine I. Podilchuk and Edward J. Delp, "Digital Watermarking: Algorithms and Applications", IEEE Signal Processing Magazine, 2001, pp. 33-46.

29. X. Kang, W. Zeng, & J. Huang, "A Multi-band Wavelet Watermarking Scheme", International Journal of Network Security, Vol. 6, No. 2, 2008, pp. 121-126.

30. M. Barni, F. Bartolini, V. Cappellini & A. Piva, "A DCT domain system for robust image watermarking", Signal Processing, Vol. 66, Issue. 3, 1998, pp. 357-372.

31. N. Suehiro, N. Kuroyanagi, T. Imoto & S. Matsufuji, "Very efficient frequency usage system using convolutional spread time signals based on complete complementary code", 11th International Symposium on Personal, Indoor and Mobile Radio Communications, Vol. 2, 2000, pp. 1567–1572.

32. J. Cox, J. Kilian, T. Leighton, & T. Shamoon, "Secure spread spectrum watermarking for images, audio and video," International Conference on Image Processing, Vol. 3, 1996, pp. 243–246.

33. C. T. Hsu & J. L. Wu, "Hidden Digital Watermarks in Images", IEEE Transactions On Image Processing, Vol. 8, Issue. 1, 1999, pp. 58-68.

34. Sarwate D.V., Pursley M.B. "Crosscorrelation Properties of Pseudorandom and Related Sequences" Proc. of the IEEE, Vol. 68, Issue. 5, 1980, pp 593-619.

35. Channapragada R. S. R. & Munaga V. N. K. Prasad, "Digital watermarking algorithm based on complete complementary code", Third International Conference on Computing Communication & Networking Technologies (ICCCNT), 2012, pp. 1-4.

36. J.F. Delaigle, C. Devleeschouwer, B. Macq & I. Langendijk, "Human visual system features enabling watermarking", IEEE International Conference on Multimedia and Expo, Vol. 2, 2002, pp. 489-492.

37. R.L. Pickholtz, D.L. Schilling, and L.B. Milstein, "Theory of spread spectrum communications – a tutorial", IEEE transactions on communications (COM-30), 1982, pp. 855-884.

38. Y. Horii & T. Kojima, "On digital watermarks based on complete complementary codes", Fourth International Workshop on Signal Design and its Applications in Communications, 2009, pp. 126–129.

39. Kojima, T., Ohtani, N., Matsumoto, T. & Parampalli, U., "A Blind Digital Watermarking Scheme Based on Complete Complementary Code", Australian Communications Theory Workshop, 2011, pp. 1-6.

40. N. Suehiro & M. Hatori, "N-shift cross-orthogonal sequences", IEEE Transactions on Information Theory, Vol. 34, Issue. 1, 1988, pp. 143–146

41. Lincong zhang, Chaoyuan tan, Hua dai, Yu wu & Bingfali, "Adaptive digital watermarking algorithm based on gold codes and wavelet transform", Book title: "Wavelet Analysis and Active Media Technology", 2005, pp. 134-139.

42. Fiebig, U. -C. G., "Auto- and cross correlation properties for extended m-sequences and related sequences", IEEE Third International Symposium on Spread Spectrum Techniques and Applications, Vol. 2, 1994, pp. 406 – 410

43. E. Koch & J. Zhao, "Embedding robust labels into images for copyright protection", International Congress on Intellectual Property Rights for Specialized Information, Knowledge & New Technologies, 1995, pp. 1-10.

44. N.F. Maxemchuk & S. Low, "Marking text documents", International Conference on Image Processing, Vol. 3, 1997, pp. 1-13.

45. Lin ET, Christine I, Podilchuk B & Delp EJ, "Detection of image alterations using semi-fragile watermarks", Proceedings of the SPIE international conference on security and water-marking of multimedia contents II, Vol. 3971, 2000, pp. 1-12.

46. Min Wu & Bede Liu, "Data Hiding in Binary Image for Authentication and Annotation", IEEE Transactions on Multimedia, Vol. 6, Issue. 4, 2004, pp. 528-538.

47. Amnach Khawne, Orachat Chitsobhuk & Toshiyuki Nakamiya, "A Study of using L1-norm with Image Watermarking on SVD Domain", Third International Conference on International Information Hiding and Multimedia Signal Processing, Vol. 2, 2007, pp. 67-70.

48. X.B. Wen, H. Zhang, X.Q. Xu & J.J. Quan, "A new watermarking approach based on proba-bilistic neural network in wavelet domain", Journal of Soft computing, Vol. 13, Issue. 4, 2008, pp. 355-360

49. Grace C.-W. Ting, Bok-Min Goi, Swee-Huay Heng, "Attack on a semi-blind watermarking scheme based on singular value decomposition". Computer Standards & Interfaces, Vol. 31, 2009, pp. 523–525.

50. Chin-Chen Chang, The Duc Kieu, Zhi-Hui Wang & Ming-Chu Li, "An Image Authentication Scheme Using Magic Square", 2nd IEEE International Conference on Computer Science and Information Technology (ICCSIT), 2009, pp. 1-4

51. Wang Jing-pei, Sun Shui-fa Jiang Ming, Xie Dan-guil & Lei Bang-jun, "Anti-protocol attacks digital watermarking Based on Media-Hash and SVD", Fifth International Conference on Information Assurance and Security, Vol. 01, 2009, pp. 364 - 367.

52. Iman Omidvar Tehrani & Subariah Ibrahim, "An Enhanced SVD Based watermarking Using U Matrix", 5th International Conference of Computer Sciences and Convergence Information Technology, 2010, pp. 627-631.

53. P Karthigaikumar & K Baskaran, "An ASIC implementation of a low power invisible robust watermarking processor", International journal of system architecture, Vol. 57, Issue. 4, 2010, pp. 404-411.

54. Afrin Zahra Husaini & M Nizamuddin, "Challenges and approach for a robust image water marking algorithm", International journal of Electronics Engineering, Vol. 2, Issue. 1, 2010, pp. 229-233.

55. Jun Wang, Hong Peng & Peng Shi, "An optimal image watermarking approach based on a multi-objective genetic algorithm", International Journal of Information Sciences, Vol. 181, Issue. 24, 2011, pp. 5501–5514

56. R. Reyes, C. Cruz, M. Nakano-Miyatake & H. Pérez-Meana, "A Digital Video Watermarking in DWT Domain Using Chaotic Mixtures", IEEE Latin America Transactions, Vol. 8, No. 3, 2011, pp. 304-310.

57. Morteza Makhloghi, Fardin Akhlaghian Tab & Habibollah Danyali, "A new robust blind DWT-SVD based digital image watermarking", 19th Iranian Conference on Electrical Engineering (ICEE), 2011, pp. 1-5.

58. Chih-Chin Lai, "A digital watermarking scheme based on singular value decomposition and tiny Genetic algorithm", Digital Signal Processing, Vol. 21, 2011, pp. 522–527.

59. Rajlaxmi Chouhan, Rajib Kumar Jha, Apoorv Chaturvedi, T. Yamasaki & K. Aizawa, "Robust Watermark Extraction using SVD based Dynamic Stochastic Resonance", International Conference of Recent Advances in Intelligent Computational Systems (RAICS), 2011, pp. 2745-2748.

60. Ray-Shine Run, Shi-Jinn Horng, Jui-Lin Lai, Tzong-Wang Kao & Rong-Jian Chen, "An improved SVD-based watermarking technique for copyright protection", Expert Systems with Applications, Vol. 39, 2011, pp. 673–689.

61. Dawen Xu, Rangding Wang & Jicheng Wang, "A novel watermarking scheme for H.264/AVC video authentication", International Journal of Signal Processing: Image Communication, Vol. 26, 2011, pp. 267–279.

62. P. Karthigaikumar, Anumol & K. Baskaran, "A FPGA implementation of high speed low area DWT based invisible image watermarking algorithm", Procedia Engineering, Vol. 30, 2012, pp. 266 – 273.

63. Zende, D.A. Chavan, M.K., "Binary image authentication using zig-zag ordering of water-mark", International Conference on Advances in Technology and Engineering (ICATE), 2013, pp. 1-5.

64. Djallel Eddine Boubiche, Sabrina Boubiche, & Azeddine Bilami, "Djallel Eddine Boubiche, Sabrina Boubiche, and Azeddine Bilami", IEEE Communications Letters, Vol. 19, No. 5, 2015, pp. 823 – 826.

65. Channapragada R. S. G. Rao, V. Ravi, Munaga V. N. K. Prasad & E. V. Gopal, "Digital Watermarking Techniques for Images – Survey", in "Encyclopedia of Business Analytics and Optimization", Eds. James W., Hershey, PA: IGI Global Publications Vol. 2, 2014, pp. 191-200.

66. Saeed Sarreshtedari, & Mohammad Ali Akhaee, "A Source-Channel Coding Approach to Digital Image Protection and Self-Recovery", IEEE Transactions on Image Processing, Vol. 24, No. 7, 2015, pp. 2266 – 2277.

67. Channapragada R. S. G. Rao, V. Ravi, Munaga V. N. K. Prasad & E. V. Gopal, "Watermarking Using Intelligent Methods - Survey", in "Encyclopedia of Business Analytics and Optimization", Eds. James W., Hershey, PA" IGI Global Publications Vol. 5, 2014, pp. 449-462.

68. G. H. Golub and C. F. V. Loan, "Matrix Computations (Johns Hopkins Studies in Mathematical Sciences)", 3rd ed.,. Johns Hopkins

69. Paquet A.H. & Ward R.K., "Wavelet-based digital watermarking for image authentication", Proceedings of the IEEE Canadian conference on electrical and computer engineering, Vol. I, 2002, pp. 879–884

70. Falkowski B.J. & Lim L.S. "Image watermarking using Hadamard transform". Electronics Letters, Vol. 36, 2000, pp. 211–213.

71. Gilani SAM & Skodras AN. "Watermarking by multi resolution Hadamard transform". Proceedings of European Conference on Electronic Imaging and Visual Arts, 2001, pp. 1-5.

72. Ho ATS, Shen J, Chow AKK & Woon J., "Robust digital image-in-image watermarking algorithm using fast Hadamard transform", Proceedings in International symposium on circuits and systems, 2003, pp. 826–829.

73. Li H, Wang S, WS & Wen Q., "Multiple watermarking using Hadamard transform", 6th International conference on Advances in Web Age Information Management, 2005, pp. 767–772.

74. Santi P. Maitya & Malay K. Kundu., "DHT domain digital watermarking with low loss in image information", International Journal of Electronics and Communications, Vol. 64, Issue. 3, 2010, pp. 243–257

75. Sarker, Md.Iqbal H. & Khan, M.I., "An improved blind watermarking method in frequency domain for image authentication", International Conference on Informatics, Electronics & Vision (ICIEV), 2013, pp. 1-5.

76. Hao-Tang Chan, Wen-Jyi Hwang, and Chau-Jern Cheng, "Digital Hologram Authentication Using a Hadamard-Based Reversible Fragile Watermarking Algorithm", Journal of Display Technology, Vol. 11, No. 2, 2015, pp. 193-203

77. H. Lu, X. Shi, Y. Q. Shi, A. C. Kot & L. Chen, "Watermark Embedding in DC Components of DCT for Binary Image", Proceedings of the IEEE International Symposium Workshop on Multimedia Signal Processing, 2002, pp. 300-303.

78. Dianwu Gao, Wei Chen, Shiyong Yang & Fusheng Feng, "Realization of Digital Watermark Technology Based on Static Image in Multimedia", International Conference on Machine Vision and Human-machine Interface, 2010, pp. 334-337.

79. Roland Hu, Fei Chen & Huimin Yu, "Incorporating Watson's perceptual model into patch-work watermarking for digital images", IEEE 17th International Conference on Image Processing, 2010, pp. 26-29.

80. Qiuping Guo Bin He Yuqian Wu, "A Creditability Validation Algorithm for Paper-based Documents", International Conference on multimedia technology (ICMT),2010, pp. 1-4.

81. Pengfei Wang & Yewang Chen, "A Fragile Watermarking Algorithm Based on Logistic System and JPEG", Science Foundation for Excellent Young Scholars of Anhui Province, 2010, pp. 663-666.

82. Reza Mortezaei & Mohsen Ebrahimi Moghaddam, "A New Lossless Watermarking Scheme Based On fuzzy integral and DCT domain", International Conference on Electronics and Information Engineering, Vol. 1, 2010, pp. V1-527-V1-531.

83. Tsou, Yao-Chun; Li, Ying, "Complete complementary code-based digital watermarking with embedding region reduction", IEEE 17th International Symposium on Consumer Electronics (ISCE), 2013, pp. 219-220.

84. http://www-history.mcs.st-and.ac.uk/Biographies/ Daubechies.html

85. Kundur D & Hatzinakos D, "Digital watermarking for telltale tamper proofing and authentication", Proceedings of IEEE, Vol. 87, Issue. 7, 2009, pp. 1167–1180.

86. Inoue H., Miyazaki A. & Katsura T., "A digital watermark for images using the wavelet transform", Integrated Computer Aided Engineering, Vol. 7, Issue. 2, 2000, pp. 105–115.

87. S. Joo, Y. Suh, J. Shin & H. Kitkuchi, "A new robust watermarking embedding in to wavelet DC components", ETRI Journal, Vol. 24, Issue. 5, 2002, pp. 401–404.

88. S.C. Chu, H.C. Huang, Y. Shi, S.Y. Wu & C.S. Shieh, "Genetic watermarking for Zerotree based applications", Circuits Systems and Signal Processing, Vol. 27, 2008, pp. 171-182

89. A.E. Hassanien, A. Abraham and C. Grosan, "Spiking neural networks and wavelets for hiding iris data in digital images", Journal soft computing, Vol. 13, Issue. 4, 2009, pp. 401-406

90. Huang Hui-fen, "Perceptual Image Watermarking Algorithm Based on Magic Squares Scrambling in DWT", 5th International Joint conference on INC, IMS, IDC, 2009, pp. 1819-1822

91. Mohamed Ouhsain & A.Ben Hamza, "Image watermarking scheme using nonnegative matrix factorization and wavelet transform", Journal of Expert Systems with Applications, Vol. 36, 2009, pp. 2123-2129.

92. Min-Jen Tsai, "A visible watermarking algorithm based on the content and contrast aware (COCOA) technique", Journal of Visual Communication and Image Representation, Vol. 20, 2009, pp. 323–338.

93. LI Hui-fang, CHANG Ning & CHEN Xiao-ming,"A study on image digital watermarking based on wavelet transform", The Journal of Universities of Posts and Telecommunications, Vol. 17, 2010, pp. 122–126.

94. Feng Shi, Yongge Shi & Lin Lai, "Optimization on Digital Watermarking Algorithm Based on SVD-DWT", IEEE International Conference on Granular Computing, 2011, pp. 582 - 585.

95. Gaurav Bhatnagar, Q.M. Jonathan Wu & Balasubramanian Raman, "Discrete fractional wavelet transform and its application to multiple encryption", International journal of Information Sciences, Vol. 223, 2013, pp. 297–316.

96. Khalili, M.; Asatryan, D, "Colour spaces effects on improved discrete wavelet transform-based digital image watermarking using Arnold transform map", IET Signal Processing, Vol. 7, Issue. 3, 2013, pp. 177-187.

97. Tiwari, N. Kumar Ramaiya, M. and Sharma, M., "Digital watermarking using DWT and DES", IEEE 3rd International on Advance Computing Conference (IACC), 2013, pp. 1100-1102.

98. Jean-Luc Starck, Emmanuel J. Candès & David L. Donoho, "The Curvelet Transform for Image Denoising", IEEE Transactions on Image Processing, Vol. 11, No. 6, 2002, pp. 670-684

99. Channapragada R. S. R. & Munaga V. N. K. Prasad, "Digital Watermarking Based on Magic Square and Ridgelet Transform Techniques", Intelligent Computing, Networking, and Informatics (International Conference on Advanced Computing, Networking and Informatics-Advances in Intelligent Systems and Computing), Vol. 243, 2014, pp. 143-161.

100. Patrizio Campisi, Deepa Kundur & Alessandro Neri, "Robust Digital Watermarking in the Ridgelet Domain", IEEE Signal Processing Letters, Vol. 11, No. 10, 2004, pp. 826-830

101. Yuancheng Li, "An Image Digital Watermarking Method Based On Ridgelet and KICA", International Conference on MultiMedia and Information Technology (MMIT), 2008, pp. 345-348

102. David L. Donoho & Ana Georgina Flesia, "Digital Ridgelet Transform based on True Ridge Functions", International Journal of Studies in Computational Mathematics, Vol. 10, 2003, pp. 1–30

103. Changjiang Zhang & Min Hu, "Curvelet Image Watermarking Using Genetic Algorithms", Congress on Image and Signal Processing, Vol. 1, 2008, pp. 486-490

104. Emil Frank Hembrooke, "Identification of sound and like signals",. United States Patent, 3,004,104,1961.

105. http://www.alpvision.com/watermarking.html

106. Ramkumar M., Akansu A.N., "Capacity estimates for data hiding in compressed images", IEEE Transactions on Image Processing, Vol. 10, Issue. 8, 2001, pp. 1252–1263.

107. Eratne, S & Alahakoon, M., "Fast Predictive Wavelet Transform for lossless image compression", Fourth International Conference on Industrial and Information Systems, 2009, pp. 365 – 368

108. Channapragada R. S. G. Rao, V. Ravi, Munaga V. N. K. Prasad & E. V. Gopal, "Watermarking Using Artificial Intelligence Techniques", in "Encyclopedia of Business Analytics and Optimization", Eds. James W., Hershey, PA: IGI Global Publications Vol. 5, 2014, pp. 436-448

109. Fitzgerald, Brian F., Shi, Sampsung Xiaoxiang, Foong, Cheryl, & Pappalardo, Kylie M., "Country of Origin and Internet Publication: Applying the Berne Convention in the Digital Age". Journal of Intellectual Property (NJIP) Maiden Edition, 2011, pp. 38-73

110. Hannibal Travis, "Opting Out of the Internet in the United States and the European Union: Copyright, Safe Harbors, and International Law", Notre Dame Law Review, Vol. 83, No. 4, 2008, pp. 331-408.

111. Barbara Fox & Brian A. LaMacchia, "Encouraging Recognition of Fair Uses in DRM Systems", Communications of ACM, Vol. 46, Issue. 4, 2003, pp. 61-63.

112. Iannella R., "Digital Rights Management (DRM) Architectures", D-Lib Magazine, Vol. 7, No. 6, 2001, pp. 1-5.

113. Praveen Dalal, "Data Protection Law in India: The TRIPS Perspective", Journal of Intellectual Property Rights, Vol. 11, 2006, pp. 125-131

Chapter 2
Color Image Watermarking Techniques Based on Magic Square and Curvelets

Abstract Four digital watermarking techniques (image watermarking using curvelet transform (WCT), watermark wavelets in curvelets of cover image (WWCT), resized watermark into curvelets of cover image (RWCT), resized watermark wavelets into curvelets of cover image (RWWCT)) based on curvelet transform are discussed in this chapter. In WCT both the embedding and extraction procedures are discussed, where the watermark is embedded into the curvelets of the color cover image. In WWCT the wavelets of watermark are obtained. These wavelets are embedded into the color image curvelets. In RWCT the watermark is resized based on magic square technique and then embedded into the color image curvelets. In RWWCT the resized watermark obtained through the magic square procedure is transformed through wavelet transformation and then the wavelets are embedded into the curvelets of the cover image. The results indicate that the embedding and extraction procedures of WWCT and RWWCT are much superior to WCT and RWCT. The regeneration of watermark image is satisfactory, but lossy.

2.1 Introduction

This chapter deals with the design, development, and implementation of the digital watermark techniques based on magic square, discrete wavelet transforms, and curvelet transform procedures for images. In the process of implementing the above techniques, it also focuses on prerequisites like magic square [1], discrete wavelet transformation [2], and curvelet transformation [3, 4]. As vision index and sensitivity of the human eye are relatively very low for blue and yellow color component [5], the watermark will be embedded in the blue component for all the techniques.

In 2009, Huang Hui-fen executed the application by using gray scale images for both host and watermark images [6]. The study obtained a new image consisting of magic square by scrambling the watermark image and embedded the same through discrete wavelet transform (DWT) technique. However, this is not tested in host color image. In 2008, Chune Zhang et al. have generated watermark image hash by

© The Author(s) 2016
C.R.S. Rao, M.V.N.K. Prasad, *Digital Watermarking Techniques in Curvelet and Ridgelet Domain*, SpringerBriefs in Computer Science, DOI 10.1007/978-3-319-32951-2_2

obtaining approximate scale through multi-scale curvelet transformations. The image features represented as bit sequences are then embedded into cover image [7]. Yuancheng Li discussed a novel algorithm based on gray scale images [8]. The watermark image is first scrambled using Arnold scrambling technique and then same is embedded using ridgelet transform technique. The extracted watermark is compared with original and calculated normalized correlation of approximately 0.9. Patrizio Campisi considered gray scale images for his results [9]. The watermark is embedded into the most significant edges of the host image with the help of ridgelet transform technique. The extracted watermark showed a high correlation of 100% for JPEG formats with 0.2-bit rates.

It is proposed to develop a technique for inserting the watermark curvatures into the cover image curvatures to secure the authentication information in the water-marked image, while the watermarked image undergoes various image compression attacks. This chapter also proposkes a technique for embedding multiple copies of the watermark through the magic square procedure.

2.1.1 Magic Square Technique

An nth order magic square is arranging n^2 distinct integers in a square, such that the sum of numbers of any row, any column or any diagonal will be the same constant [1]. The magic square is a part of Indian culture from the times of Vedic days, for example the Ganesh Yantra. The 4×4 magic square of tenth century existing in Khajuraho, Parshvanath Jain temple, India, is a popular magic square [10]. Figure 2.1 represents an example of 4×4 magic square [11, 12].

Fig. 2.1 4×4 magic square

34	34	34	34	34	34
34	1	13	12	8	
34	2	14	7	11	
34	15	3	10	6	
34	16	4	5	9	

2.2   Image Watermarking Using Curvelet Transform

This section discusses two methods in which watermark can be embedded into the curvelets of the cover image. In the first method, WCT, the watermark is embedded into cover image curvelets. In the second method, WWCT, the wavelet coefficients of watermark are embedded into the curvelets of cover image [12].

2.2.1   Technique to Insert Watermark in Curvelets of Cover Image (WCT)

In this method the watermark is segmented into nonoverlapping partitions where each partition size is p×p pixels. Similarly, cover image also partitioned and curvelets are obtained for each partition. The watermark partitions are embedded into the curvelets as discussed in Sect. 2.2.1.1. Similarly, watermarked image is partitioned and then the watermark is extracted from the curvelets of the respective partitions as discussed in Sect. 2.2.1.2. The architecture of the watermark embedding procedure is shown in Fig. 2.2 and the architecture of the extraction procedure is shown in Fig. 2.3 [12].

2.2.1.1   Digital Watermark Embedding Procedure

The detailed procedure with reference to Fig. 2.2 for embedding watermark is dis-cussed as follows.

Step 1: The third dimension or blue component of the image, CI, is partitioned into CI1 nonoverlapping blocks of p×p (for example 8×8 size) pixels in each.

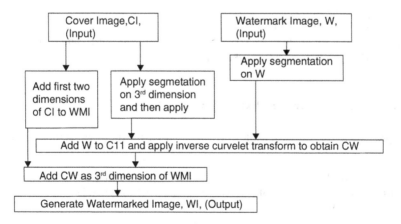

Fig. 2.2 WCT-digital watermark embedding procedure

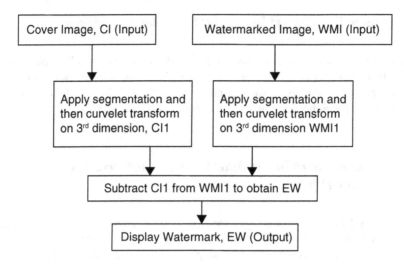

Fig. 2.3 WCT-digital watermark extraction procedure

Step 2: W is partitioned into W1 small blocks, where the size of each block is p × p pixels (for example 8 × 8 size).

Step 3: The curvelet procedure is applied to a block from CI1 to obtain curvelet coefficients, CC.

Step 4: W1 is added to the CC, using Eq. 2.1.

$$R = W1 + CC \qquad (2.1)$$

Step 5: The inverse curvelet transform procedure is applied to R and the block is added to the respective location of CC1.

Step 6: Step 5 to Step 7 are applied repeatedly till all the blocks of W1 add to respective blocks of CI1.

Step 7: Add the remaining blocks of CI1 to CC1.

Step 8: Add red and green planes of CI to resultant image, WMI, and then add CC1 to WMI to generate a watermarked image.

2.2.1.2 Digital Watermark Extraction Procedure

The procedure for extraction of watermark based on the architecture shown in Fig. 2.3 is as follows.

Step 1: The third dimension or blue component of watermarked image, WMI, is partitioned into a number of p × p (for example 8 × 8 size) pixel sized nonoverlapping blocks, WMI1.

Step 2: The third dimension or blue component of cover image, CI, is partitioned into a number of p × p pixel sized nonoverlapping blocks, CI1.

Step 3: The curvelet transformation is applied to a block from CI1 to obtain curvelet coefficients C1.

Step 4: The curvelet transformation is applied to a block from WMI1 to obtain curvelet coefficients WM1.

Step 5: Subtract the values of C1 from WM1 to obtain a block of extracting a watermark image, EWM.

Step 6: Repeat Step 5 to Step 7 for a size of given watermark (Since the watermark is embedded in continuous locations).

Step 7: Compare the extracted watermark EWM with W.

2.2.1.3   Experimental Results

A Lenna color image (Fig. 2.4a) of size 512×512 pixels is considered as the cover image, CI. A grayscale image with 64×64 pixels size is considered as watermark, W (Fig. 2.4b). The block size is considered as 8×8 pixels. The values of W are embedded with the pixel values of CI as discussed in the embedding procedure Sect. 2.2.1.1. Figure 2.5a shows the resultant watermarked image obtained through the embedding procedure. The extraction procedure discussed in Sect. 2.2.1.2 is applied on Fig. 2.5a and the watermark is extracted as shown in Fig. 2.5b and compared with the original watermark [12].

The watermark is embedded into various 24-bit standard 512×512 pixel color images, like Baboon, Pepper, and Barbara, and the respective watermarked images are generated. Table 2.1 gives the results of peak signal to noise ratio (PSNR) obtained when these watermarked images are compared with the respective cover images. From the results it is observable that the results of the WCT discussed in Sect. 2.2.1 are better than Yuancheng Li's method [8]. The results are comparable to the results obtained by Chune Zhang [7].

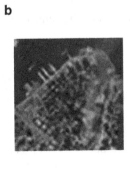

Fig. 2.4   (a) Lenna cover image. (b) Original watermark (64×64 pixels)

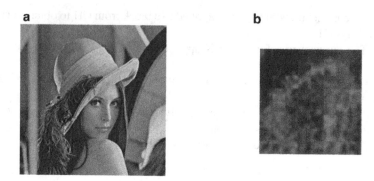

Fig. 2.5 (**a**) Watermarked Lenna BMP Image (WCT). (**b**) Extracted watermark from Fig. 2.4 (WCT)

Table 2.1 PSNR results for various cover images (WCT)

S. No.	Image name (size 512×512)	WCT	Huang Hui-fen [6]	Yuancheng Li [8]	Patrizio Campisi [9]	Chune Zhang [7]
1	Lenna	31.49	39.9	27.7	40.46	43.166
2	Baboon	31.17	–	–	37.6	–
3	Barbara	31.30	–	–	40.14	–
4	Pepper	31.20	–	–	–	–

The Lenna watermarked image (BMP image file) shown in Fig. 2.5a is compressed with GIF, JPEG, and PNG compression techniques and the resulting watermarked images are shown in Figs. 2.6, 2.8, and 2.10, respectively. Similarly the watermark is extracted from these compressed images as discussed in the procedure Sect. 2.2.1.2 and the results are shown in Figs. 2.7, 2.9, and 2.11, respectively. The technique is tested for its performance by comparing the extracted watermark with the original watermark (Fig. 2.4b) and the PSNR results are tabulated in Table 2.2. The resultant PSNR shows that the obtained watermarks are consisting of more noise [12].

2.2.2 Technique to Insert Watermark Wavelets in Curvelets of Cover Image (WWCT)

The watermark embedding and the extraction procedures are given in Figs. 2.12 and 2.13 respectively. In this method the watermark is segmented into W1 non-overlapping partitions, where each partition size is p × p pixels. The cover image is also partitioned similarly and curvelets are obtained for every partition. The wavelet coefficients of watermark partitions are embedded into the obtained

Fig. 2.6 Watermarked
Lenna image compressed
by GIF format (WCT)

Fig. 2.7 Extracted
watermark from Fig. 2.6
(WCT)

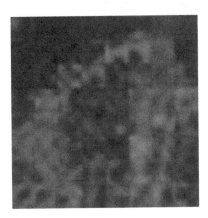

Fig. 2.8 Watermarked
Lenna image compressed
by JPEG format (WCT)

Fig. 2.9 Extracted
watermark from Fig. 2.8
(WCT)

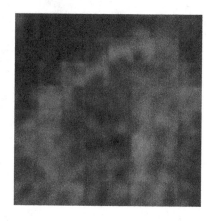

Fig. 2.10 Watermarked
Lenna image compressed
by PNG format (WCT)

Fig. 2.11 Extracted
watermark from Fig. 2.10
(WCT)

Table 2.2 Variation of PSNR for different compression formats (WCT)

S. No.	Type of attack on 24-bit color Lenna image (size 512×512)	PSNR obtained
1	Watermark extracted from BMP image	21.53
2	Bmp converted to GIF format	21.41
3	Bmp converted to JPEG format	20.39
4	Bmp converted to PNG format	21.42

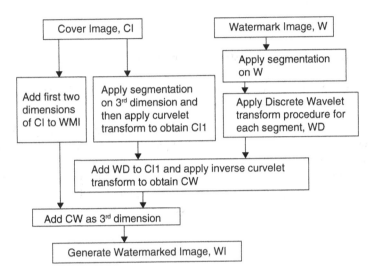

Fig. 2.12 WWCT-digital watermark embedding procedure

curvelets as discussed in Sect. 2.2.2.1. In the same way the watermarked image is partitioned into WMI1 blocks and then the watermark is extracted from the curvelets of the respective blocks as discussed in Sect. 2.2.2.2 [12].

2.2.2.1   Digital Watermark Embedding Procedure

The architecture of embedding procedure is given in Fig. 2.12 and the detailed steps for embedding watermark are as follows:

Step 1: The third dimension or blue component of the image, CI, is partitioned into a number of p×p pixel sized nonoverlapping blocks, CI1.

Step 2: W is partitioned into a number of small blocks, where the size of each block is p×p pixels, W1.

Step 3: The curvelet procedure is applied to a block from CI1 to obtain curvelet coefficients, CC.

Step 4: The discrete wavelet transform procedure is applied to a block from W1 to obtain transform coefficients, WD.

Step 5: WD is added to the CC, using Eq. 2.1.

Step 6: The inverse curvelet transform procedure is applied on R and the block is added to respective location of CC1.

Step 7: Step 3 to Step 6 are repeated till all the blocks of W1 are added to respective blocks of CI1.

Step 8: Add the remaining blocks of CI1 to CC1.

Step 9: Add red and green planes of CI to WMI and then add CC1 to WMI to generate watermarked image.

2.2.2.2 Digital Watermark Extraction Procedure

The architecture of extraction procedure is given in Fig. 2.13 and the detailed steps for extraction of the watermark are as follows:

Step 1: The third dimension or blue component of watermarked image, WMI, is partitioned into a number of $p \times p$ (for example 8×8 size) pixel sized nonoverlapping blocks, WMI1.

Step 2: The third dimension or blue component of cover image, CI, is partitioned into a number of $p \times p$ pixel sized nonoverlapping blocks, CI1.

Step 3: The curvelet transformation is applied to a block from CI1 to obtain curvelet coefficients C1.

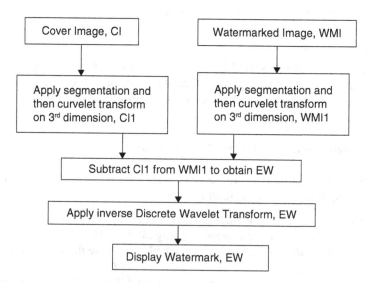

Fig. 2.13 WWCT-digital watermark extraction procedure

Step 4: The curvelet transformation is applied to a block from WMI1 to obtain curvelet coefficients WM1.

Step 5: Subtract the values of C1 from WM1 and apply inverse discrete wavelet transform procedure to obtain a block of extracting a watermark image, EWM.

Step 6: Repeat Step 3 to Step 5 for a size of given watermark (Since the watermark is embedded in continuous locations).

Step 7: Compare the extracted watermark, EWM, with W.

2.2.2.3 Experimental Results

A Lenna color image (Fig. 2.4a) of size 512×512 pixels is considered as the cover image, CI. A gray scale image with 64×64 pixels size is considered as watermark, W (Fig. 2.4b). The block size is considered as 8×8 pixels. The values of CI are embedded with content of W as given in the embedding procedure Sect. 2.2.2.1. The resultant watermarked image after manipulation is shown in Fig. 2.14. The watermark is extracted from the watermarked image (Fig. 2.14) by following the steps discussed in the extraction procedure Sect. 2.2.2.2. The extracted watermark is as shown in Fig. 2.15. The watermark is compared with the original watermark to find the performance of the procedures [12].

The watermark is embedded into various 24-bit standard 512×512 pixel color images and the respective watermarked images are generated. Table 2.3 gives the results of PSNR obtained when these watermarked images are compared with the

Fig. 2.14 Watermarked Lenna BMP image (WWCT)

Fig. 2.15 Extracted
watermark from Fig. 2.14
(WWCT)

Table 2.3 PSNR results for various cover images (WWCT)

S. No.	Image name (size 512×512)	WWCT	Huang Hui-fen [6]	Yuancheng Li [8]	Patrizio Campisi [9]	Chune Zhang [7]
1	Lenna	42.09	39.9	27.7	40.46	43.166
2	Baboon	36.19	–	–	37.6	–
3	Barbara	39.68	–	–	40.14	–
4	Pepper	39.14	–	–	–	–

respective cover images. The results show that the performance of the technique discussed is better than the methods discussed by Huang Hui-fen [6], Yuancheng Li [8], Patrizio Campisi [9] and are comparable to the results obtained by Chune Zhang [7].

The Lenna watermarked image (BMP image file) shown in Fig. 2.14 is compressed with GIF, JPEG, and PNG compression techniques and the resulting watermarked images are shown in Figs. 2.16, 2.18, and 2.20, respectively. Similarly the watermark is extracted from these compressed images as discussed in the procedure Sect. 2.2.2.2 and the results are shown in Figs. 2.17, 2.19, and 2.21, respectively [12].

The technique is tested for its performance by comparing the extracted watermark with the original watermark (Fig. 2.4b) and the PSNR results are tabulated in Table 2.4. The resultant PSNR shows that the obtained watermarks are consisting of less noise and are in an acceptable range.

Fig. 2.16 Watermarked
Lenna image compressed
by GIF format (WWCT)

Fig. 2.17 Extracted
watermark from Fig. 2.16
(WWCT)

Fig. 2.18 Watermarked
Lenna image compressed
by JPEG format (WWCT)

Fig. 2.19 Extracted
watermark from Fig. 2.18
(WWCT)

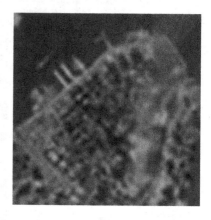

Fig. 2.20 Watermarked
Lenna image compressed
by PNG format (WWCT)

Fig. 2.21 Extracted
watermark from Fig. 2.20
(WWCT)

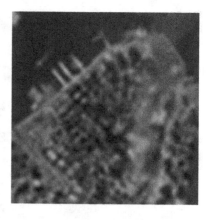

Table 2.4 Variation of PSNR for different compression formats (WWCT)

S. No.	Type of attack on 24-bit color Lenna image (size 512×512)	PSNR obtained
		WWCT
1	Watermark extracted from BMP image	34.65
2	Bmp converted to GIF format	33.27
3	Bmp converted to JPEG format	32.76
4	Bmp converted to PNG format	34.65

2.3   Image Watermarking Using Magic Square and Curvelet Transform

This section discusses about two methods in which the resized watermark is embedded into the curvelets of the cover image. The watermark is resized by using the magic square technique. In the first method, RWCT, one quadrant of the resized watermark is embedded into the cover image curvelets. In the second method, RWWCT, one quadrant of the resized watermark is transformed using discrete wavelet transform. The obtained wavelet coefficients are embedded into the curvelets of cover image [11, 12].

2.3.1   Magic Square

2.3.1.1   Magic Square Procedure

The following procedure is used to resize the watermark image (W) of size $m \times m$ pixels to equivalent cover image (CI) size of $N \times N$.

Step 1: Divide the $N \times N$ with $m \times m$ to obtain $k \times k$, the size of magic square to be generated for each pixel, i.e., for every pixel value of watermark a $k \times k$ magic square is generated.

Step 2: These $k \times k$ values will be copied to the respective positions of $k \times k$ nonoverlapping blocks.

Step 3: All the obtained magic square blocks will be positioned to obtain a watermark image IM, with size $N \times N$.

Step 4: An adjustment value array will be generated where ever the pixel value is less than the possible magic square minimum value. For example the minimum value for any 4×4 magic square is 34 so if the pixel value is less than 34 then the magic square cannot be generated. In this case the adjustment value is generated and inserted into adjustment array, AD [11, 12].

Step 5: Store AD and IM for extraction purpose.

2.3.1.2 Application

The 8×8 magic square can be treated as replication of four 4×4 magic squares for simplicity, as shown in Fig. 2.22 [11, 12].

The elements of the magic square are generated based on the Eqs. 3.2 and 2.3. In Eq. 2.2, a(1) is representing first elements value and max is the pixel value for which the 8×8 magic square to be generated.

$$a(1) = \left(\frac{(\max - 34)}{2} \right) + 1 \tag{2.2}$$

$$a(k) = (k - 1) + 1 \tag{2.3}$$

2.3.2 Technique to Insert Resized Watermark into Curvelets of Cover Image (RWCT)

In this method, the resized watermark pixel values are embedded into the curvelet partitions of cover image as discussed in Sect. 2.3.2.1. The watermark is extracted from the watermarked image curvelets as discussed in Sect. 2.3.2.2. The architecture of embedding and extraction procedures is as shown in Figs. 2.23 and 2.24 respectively [12].

2.3.2.1 Digital Watermark Embedding Procedure

The steps involved in embedding resized watermark into curvelets of cover image based on the given architecture shown in Fig. 2.23 are as follows:

Step 1: The third dimension or blue component of image, CI, is partitioned into a number of $p \times p$ (for example 8×8 size) pixel sized nonoverlapping blocks, CI1.

Step 2: Apply magic square procedure discussed in Sect. 2.3.1.1 on W to obtain IM with size equal to CI.

Step 3: One quadrant of IM is partitioned into number of nonoverlapping small blocks, where the size of each block is $p \times p$ pixels, W1.

Step 4: The curvelet procedure is applied on a block from CI1 to obtain curvelet coefficients, CC.

Step 5: W1 is added to CC, using Eq. 2.4.

$$R_{i,j} = W1_{i,j} + CC_{i,j} \tag{2.4}$$

Fig. 2.22 8×8 Magic
square format

68	68	68	68	68	68	68	68	68	68
68	1	13	12	8	8	11	6	9	
68	2	14	7	11	12	7	10	5	
68	15	3	10	6	13	14	3	4	
68	16	4	5	9	1	2	15	16	
68	8	11	6	9	1	13	12	8	
68	12	7	10	5	2	14	7	11	
68	13	14	3	4	15	3	10	6	
68	1	2	15	16	16	4	5	9	

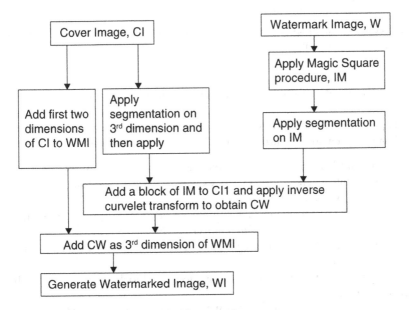

Fig. 2.23 RWCT-digital watermark embedding procedure

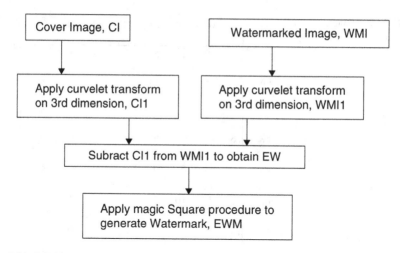

Fig. 2.24 RWCT-digital watermark extraction procedure

Step 6: The inverse curvelet transform procedure is applied on R and the block is added to respective location of CC1.

Step 7: Step 3 to Step 6 are repeated till all the blocks of W1 are added to respective blocks of CI1.

Step 8: Add the remaining blocks of CI1 to CC1.

Step 9: Add red and green planes of CI to WMI and then add CC1 to WMI to generate watermarked image.

2.3.2.2   Digital Watermark Extraction Procedure

The steps involved in extracting watermark from curvelets of watermarked image based on the given architecture shown in Fig. 2.24 are as follows:

Step 1: The third dimension or blue component of watermarked image, WMI, is partitioned into a number of $p \times p$ (for example 8×8 size) pixel sized nonoverlapping blocks, WMI1.

Step 2: The third dimension or blue component of cover image, CI, is partitioned into a number of $p \times p$ pixel sized nonoverlapping blocks, CI1.

Step 3: The curvelet transformation is applied to a block from CI1 to obtain curvelet coefficients C1.

Step 4: The curvelet transformation is applied to a block from WMI1 to obtain curvelet coefficients WM1.

Step 5: Subtract the values of C1 from WM1 to obtain a block of EM.

Step 6: Repeat Step 3 to Step 5 for a one quadrant (Since one quadrant of the magic square is embedded in continuous locations), EM.

Step 7: Generate the watermark based on magic square technique (the sum of all elements in any row, column, or diagonal will give the respective pixel value), EWM

Step 8: Compare the extracted watermark EWM with W.

2.3.2.3 Experimental Results

A Lenna color image (Fig. 2.4a) of size 512×512 pixels is considered as the cover image, CI. The block size is considered as 8×8 pixels. An array, IM, of a size equivalent to the size of cover image is created with all zero values initially and divided into 64 equal nonoverlapping blocks. A grayscale image with 64×64 pixels size is considered as watermark, W (Fig. 2.4b). The magic square application discussed in Sect. 2.3.1.2 is applied on each pixel of W to generate a magic square for the given pixel value. The 64 elements of the obtained magic square are inserted into all blocks of IM at the respective pixel location as considered from W. This results in resized watermark consisting of 64 blocks of the given watermark with varying intensities and the image is shown in Fig. 2.25. Figure 2.26 is obtained by scaling the Fig. 2.25 by a factor of 10. The minimum value is 34 for which a 4×4 magic square can be generated. As per the magic square procedure discussed in Sect. 2.3.1.2, for all pixels of W an adjustment array, AD, is generated [12].

The embedding procedure discussed in Sect. 2.3.2.1 is applied. The resultant watermarked image of the embedding procedure is shown in Fig. 2.27. The watermark is extracted from the watermarked image (Fig. 2.27) as discussed in the procedure Sect. 2.3.2.2 and is shown in Fig. 2.28. The result is compared with the original watermark to check the performance of the technique.

The watermark is embedded into various 24-bit standard color images and tested for the performance. Table 2.5 gives the comparison between cover images and watermarked images based on PSNR. The PSNR shows that the obtained watermarked images are noisy images. It is observable that the technique is better than Yuancheng Li's watermarking technique [8] and comparable to Chune Zhang et al. watermarking Technique [7].

The Lenna watermarked image (BMP image file) shown in Fig. 2.27 is compressed with GIF, JPEG, and PNG compression techniques and the resulting watermarked images are shown in Figs. 2.29, 2.31, and 2.33, respectively. Similarly the watermark is extracted from these compressed images as discussed in the procedure Sect. 2.3.2.2 and the results are shown in Figs. 2.30, 2.32, and 2.34, respectively [12].

Fig. 2.25 Resized watermark (RWCT)

Fig. 2.26 Resized
watermark scaled with 10
factor (RWCT)

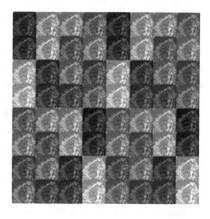

Fig. 2.27 Watermarked
Lenna BMP image
(RWCT)

Fig. 2.28 Extracted
watermark from Fig. 2.27
(RWCT)

Table 2.5 PSNR results for various cover images (RWCT)

S. No	Image name (size 512×512)	RWCT	Huang Hui-fen [6]	Yuancheng Li [8]	Patrizio Campisi [9]	Bhatnagar [13]	Chune Zhang [7]
1	Lenna	32.35	39.9	27.7	40.46	39.65	43.166
2	Baboon	31.50	–	–	37.6	–	–
3	Barbara	31.63	–	–	40.14	–	–
4	Pepper	31.52	–	–	–	–	–

Fig. 2.29 Watermarked Lenna image compressed by GIF format (RWCT)

Fig. 2.30 Extracted watermark from Fig. 2.29 (RWCT)

Fig. 2.31 Watermarked
Lenna image compressed
by JPEG format (RWCT)

Fig. 2.32 Extracted
watermark from Fig. 2.31
(RWCT)

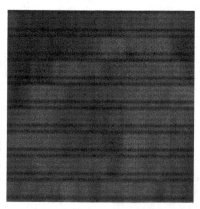

Fig. 2.33 Watermarked
Lenna image compressed
by PNG format (RWCT)

Fig. 2.34 Extracted
watermark from Fig. 2.33
(RWCT)

The technique is tested for its performance by comparing the extracted watermarks with the original watermark (Fig. 2.4b) and the PSNR results are tabulated in Table 2.6. The resultant PSNR shows that the obtained watermarks are noisy. So there is a need to strengthen the technique.

2.3.3   Technique to Insert Resized Watermark Wavelets into Curvelets of Cover Image (RWWCT)

The architectures of embedding and extraction procedures of this technique are as shown in Figs. 2.35 and 2.36 respectively. In this method, the watermark is resized by using the magic square procedure as discussed in Sect. 2.3.1. One quadrant of the magic square is considered and segmented into W1 nonoverlapping partitions, where each partition size is $p \times p$ pixels, and DWT is applied to each partition. The cover image is also partitioned similarly and curvelets are calculated for every partition. The wavelets of magic square partitions are embedded into the obtained curvelets as given in the embedding procedure Sect. 2.3.1.1. In the same way the watermarked image is partitioned into WMI1 blocks and then the watermark is extracted from the curvelets of the respective blocks as discussed in Sect. 2.3.1.2 [12].

2.3.3.1   Digital Watermark Embedding Procedure

The steps involved in embedding wavelets of resized watermark into curvelets of cover image based on the given architecture shown in Fig. 2.35 are as follows:

Step 1: The third dimension or blue component of image, CI, is partitioned into a number of $p \times p$ (for example 8×8 size) pixel sized nonoverlapping blocks, CI1.

Step 2: Apply magic square procedure discussed in Sect. 2.3.1 on W to obtain IM with size equal to CI.

Table 2.6 Variation of PSNR for different compression formats (RWCT)

S. No.	Type of attack on 24-bit color Lenna image (size 512×512)	PSNR obtained
		RWCT
1	Watermark extracted from BMP image	15.64
2	Bmp converted to GIF format	15.65
3	Bmp converted to JPEG format	14.89
4	Bmp converted to PNG format	15.64

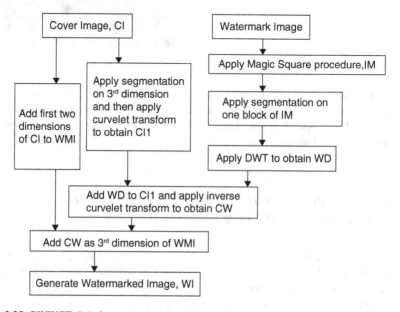

Fig. 2.35 RWWCT-digital watermark embedding procedure

Step 3: One quadrant of IM is partitioned into a number of nonoverlapping small blocks, where the size of each block is p×p pixels, W1.

Step 4: The curvelet procedure is applied to a block from CI1 to obtain curvelet coefficients, CC.

Step 5: The discrete wavelet transform procedure is applied to a block from W1 to obtain transform coefficients, WD.

Step 6: WD is added to the CC, using Eq. 2.5.

$$R_{i,j} = WD_{i,j} + CC_{i,j} \qquad (2.5)$$

Step 7: The inverse curvelet transform procedure is applied to R and the block is added to respective location of CC1.

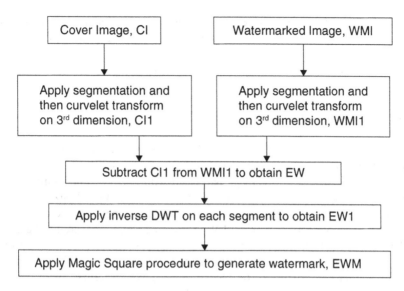

Fig. 2.36 RWWCT-digital watermark extraction procedure

Step 8: Step 3 to Step 7 are repeated till all the blocks of W1 add to respective blocks of CI1.

Step 9: Add the remaining blocks of CI1 to CC1.

Step 10: Add red and green planes of CI to WMI and then add CC1 to WMI to generate a watermarked image.

2.3.3.2   Digital Watermark Extraction Procedure

The steps involved in extracting watermark from curvelets of cover image based on the given architecture shown in Fig. 2.36 are as follows:

Step 1: The third dimension or blue component of watermarked image, WMI, is partitioned into a number of $p \times p$ (for example 8×8 size) pixel sized nonoverlapping blocks, WMI1.

Step 2: The third dimension or blue component of cover image, CI, is partitioned into a number of $p \times p$ pixel sized nonoverlapping blocks, CI1.

Step 3: The curvelet transformation is applied to a block from CI1 to obtain curvelet coefficients C1.

Step 4: The curvelet transformation is applied to a block from WMI1 to obtain curvelet coefficients WM1.

Step 5: Subtract the values of C1 from WM1 and apply inverse wavelet transform to obtain a block of EM.

Step 6: Repeat Step 3 to Step 5 for a one quadrant (Since one quadrant of the magic square is embedded in continuous locations), EM.

Step 7: Generate the watermark based on magic square technique (the sum of all elements in any row, column or diagonal will give the respective pixel value), EWM

Step 8: Compare the extracted watermark EWM with W.

2.3.3.3 Experimental Results

A Lenna color image (Fig. 2.4a) of size 512×512 pixels is considered as a cover image, CI. The block size is considered as 8×8 pixels. An array, IM, of a size equivalent to the size of cover image is created with all zero values initially and divided into 64 equal blocks. A grayscale image with 64×64 pixels size is considered as watermark, W (Fig. 2.4b). The magic square application discussed in Sect. 2.3.1.2 is applied to each pixel of W to generate a magic square for the given pixel value. The 64 elements of the obtained magic square are inserted into all blocks of IM at the respective pixel location as considered from W. This results in resized watermark consisting of 64 blocks of the given watermark with varying intensities and the image is shown in Fig. 2.25. Figure 2.26 is the complement image of Fig. 2.25. The minimum value is 34 for which a 4×4 magic square can be generated. As per the magic square procedure discussed in Sect. 2.3.1.2, for all pixels of W an adjustment array, AD, is generated [11, 12].

The embedding procedure discussed in Sect. 2.3.3.1 is applied. The resultant watermarked image of the embedding procedure is shown in Fig. 2.37. The watermark is extracted from the watermarked image (Fig. 2.37) as discussed in the procedure Sect. 2.3.3.2 and is shown in Fig. 2.38. The result is compared with the original watermark to check the performance of the technique.

The watermark is embedded into various 24-bit color images and they are compared. Table 2.7 gives the comparison between cover images and watermarked images based on PSNR. The results show that the technique is better than the techniques discussed by Huang Hui-fen [6], Yuancheng Li [8], and Patrizio Campisi [9] in the case of the Lenna cover image. The technique has shown its weakness when compared with Patrizio Campisi [9] technique in the cases of Baboon and Barbara cover images and also in the case of technique discussed by Chune Zhang [7].

The Lenna watermarked image (BMP image file) shown in Fig. 2.37 is compressed with GIF, JPEG, and PNG compression techniques and the resultant watermarked images are shown in Figs. 2.39, 2.41, and 2.43, respectively. Similarly the watermark is extracted from these compressed images as discussed in the procedure Sect. 2.3.3.2 and the results are shown in Figs. 2.40, 2.42, and 2.44, respectively [12].

The technique is tested for its performance by comparing the extracted watermark with the original watermark (Fig. 2.4b) and the PSNR results are tabulated in Table 2.8. The resultant PSNR shows that the obtained watermarks are noisy, but are in acceptable level. There is a possibility to improve the quality of extracting watermark by improving the technique.

Fig. 2.37 Watermarked
Lenna BMP image
(RWWCT)

Fig. 2.38 Extracted
watermark from Fig. 2.37
(RWWCT)

Table 2.7 PSNR results for various cover images (RWWCT)

S. No	Image name (size 512×512)	RWWCT	Huang Hui-fen [6]	Yuancheng Li [8]	Patrizio Campisi [9]	Chune Zhang [7]
1	Lenna	42.10	39.9	27.7	40.46	43.166
2	Baboon	36.21	–	–	37.6	–
3	Barbara	39.68	–	–	40.14	–
4	Pepper	39.23	–	–	–	–

Fig. 2.39 Watermarked
Lenna image compressed
by GIF format (RWWCT)

Fig. 2.40 Extracted
watermark from Fig. 2.39
(RWWCT)

Fig. 2.41 Watermarked
Lenna image compressed
by JPEG format
(RWWCT)

Fig. 2.42 Extracted
watermark from Fig. 2.41
(RWWCT)

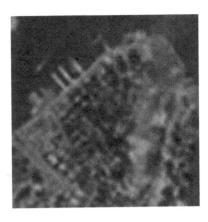

Fig. 2.43 Watermarked
Lenna image compressed
by PNG format (RWWCT)

Fig. 2.44 Extracted
watermark from Fig. 2.43
(RWWCT)

Table 2.8 Variation of PSNR for different compression formats (RWWCT)

S. No.	Type of attack on 24-bit color Lenna image (size 512×512)	PSNR obtained
1	Watermark extracted from BMP image	29.768
2	Bmp converted to GIF format	29.488
3	Bmp converted to JPEG format	29.613
4	Bmp converted to PNG format	29.768

Table 2.9 PSNR results for various cover images—Curvelet techniques

Image name (size 512× 512)	WCT	WWCT	RWCT	RWWCT	Huang Hui-fen [6]	Yuan cheng Li [8]	Patrizio Campisi [9]	Chune Zhang [7]
Lenna	31.49	42.09	32.35	42.10	39.9	27.7	40.46	43.166
Baboon	31.17	36.19	31.50	36.21	–	–	37.6	–
Barbara	31.30	39.68	31.63	39.68	–	–	40.14	–
Pepper	31.20	39.14	31.52	39.23	–	–	–	–

2.4 Summary

This chapter has presented four different methods of embedding and extraction of watermark using magic square technique and curvelet transform techniques. Table 2.9 gives the PSNR of the various watermarked image compared with the respective cover images. The current study also gives the comparative study of the extracted watermark with the original watermark (Fig. 2.4b) and the results are shown in Table 2.10. It is shown that the magic square technique can serve better in resizing the watermark image as per the requirement by spreading its brightness to create multiple copies of given watermark so as to preserve the quality of the cover image. It has also been shown that this makes the watermark to survive against compression attacks. It is observed that the technique in which the wavelet coefficients embedded in image curvelets is more efficient in retaining the watermark. The results show that the WWCT and RWWCT are better than other methods, where as WWCT is an acceptable method for preserving authentication information, i.e., for extracting less noisy watermark than other methods [12]. It is also observed that the curvelet transform techniques have demonstrated the robustness against compression attacks. But there is still scope to improve the embedding and extraction procedures, which are discussed in the next chapter.

Table 2.10 Variation of PSNR for different compression formats—Curvelet techniques

S. No.	Type of attack on 24-bit color Lenna image (size 512×512)	PSNR obtained			
		WCT	WWCT	RWCT	RWWCT
1	Watermark extracted from BMP image	21.53	34.65	15.64	29.76
2	Bmp converted to GIF format	21.41	33.27	15.65	29.48
3	Bmp converted to JPEG format	20.39	32.76	14.89	29.61
4	Bmp converted to PNG format	21.42	34.65	15.64	29.76

References

1. Tao Xie, "An evolutionary algorithm for magic squares", The 2003 congress on Evolutionary Computation, Vol. 2, 2003, pp. 906–913
2. http://www-history.mcs.st-and.ac.uk/Biographies/Daubechies.html
3. David L. Donoho & Ana Georgina Flesia, "Digital Ridgelet Transform based on True Ridge Functions", International Journal of Studies in Computational Mathematics, Vol. 10, 2003, pp. 1–30
4. Jean-Luc Starck, Emmanuel J. Candès & David L. Donoho, "The Curvelet Transform for Image Denoising", IEEE Transactions on Image Processing, Vol. 11, No. 6, 2002, pp. 670-684
5. William Symes Andrews, Lorraine Screven Frierson, Charles Albert Browne, "Magic Squares and Cubes", Chicago, IL: Open court publish company, 1908.
6. Huang Hui-fen, "Perceptual Image Watermarking Algorithm Based on Magic Squares Scrambling in DWT", 5th International Joint conference on INC, IMS, IDC, 2009, pp. 1819-1822
7. Chune Zhang, L. L. Cheng, Zhengding Qiu, and L. M. Cheng, "Multipurpose Watermarking Based on Multiscale Curvelet Transform", IEEE Transactions on Information Forensics and Security, Dec 2008, Vol. 3, No. 4, pp. 611-619.
8. Yuancheng Li, "An Image Digital Watermarking Method Based On Ridgelet and KICA", International Conference on MultiMedia and Information Technology (MMIT), 2008, pp. 345-348
9. Patrizio Campisi, Deepa Kundur & Alessandro Neri, "Robust Digital Watermarking in the Ridgelet Domain", IEEE Signal Processing Letters, Vol. 11, No. 10, 2004, pp. 826-830
10. B.A. Wandell, "Foundations of Vision", Sunderland, MA, Sinauer Associates, 1995.
11. Channapragada R. S. R. & Munaga V. N. K. Prasad, "Digital Watermarking Based on Magic Square and Ridgelet Transform Techniques", Intelligent Computing, Networking, and Informatics (International Conference on Advanced Computing, Networking and Informatics-Advances in Intelligent Systems and Computing), Vol. 243, 2014, pp. 143-161.
12. Channapragada R. S. R. & Munaga V. N. K. Prasad, "Watermarking Techniques in Curvelet Domain", International Conference on Computational Intelligence in Data Mining, Vol. 1, 2014, pp. 199-211.
13. G. Bhatnagar, B. Raman & Q.M.J. Wu, "Robust watermarking using fractional wavelet packet transform", IET Image Processing, Vol. 6, Issue. 4, 2012, pp. 386–397

Chapter 3
Color Image Watermarking Techniques Based on Magic Square and Ridgelets

Abstract Two techniques, namely image watermarking based on magic square (MST) and Image watermarking based on magic square and ridgelet transform (MSRTT), are discussed in this chapter. In the MST the watermark image is resized through the magic square procedure and is embedded into the color cover image. In MSRTT the resized watermark is transformed by ridgelet transformation. The color cover image is also transformed by the ridgelet transformation to obtain cells consisting of displacement and angle. The displacement values of watermark cells are added to cover image displacement values and the watermarked image generated. The results indicate that the embedding and extraction procedures of MSRTT are superior to MST. The regeneration of watermark image is satisfactory, but noisy.

3.1 Introduction

This chapter deals with the design and development of digital watermarking techniques based on magic square and ridgelet transform [1, 2] procedures for images. The chapter briefly discusses the prerequisite ridgelet transformation for understanding the proposed digital watermarking techniques.

In 2004, Patrizio Campisi et al. discussed a method in which the watermark is embedded into the most significant edges of the gray scale cover image with the help of ridgelet transform technique [3]. The authors chose to capture the edges of an image by decomposing it through a low-pass filter and then through a first-order filter. The resultant edge image was segmented first into blocks such that the curved edge width appears to be straight and then ridgelet transform was applied on each block. The direction having the greater energy is selected from each block and marked with a random generated mark. The inverse ridgelet transform is finally performed to obtain the marked magnitude of the edge image. The technique results have shown that the watermark embedded in edges has robustness against attacks. In 2008, Yuancheng Li discussed a method to embed Arnold scrambled watermark into a grayscale image by using ridgelet transform technique [4]. However, this

© The Author(s) 2016
C.R.S. Rao, M.V.N.K. Prasad, *Digital Watermarking Techniques
in Curvelet and Ridgelet Domain*, SpringerBriefs in Computer Science,
DOI 10.1007/978-3-319-32951-2_3

technique is not tested for color images. This chapter proposes a technique for embedding multiple copies of the watermark through the magic square procedure in ridgelet transform domain.

3.2   Image Watermarking Based on Magic Square (MST)

Figure 3.1 explains the watermark embedding procedure and Fig. 3.2 explains the extraction procedure. The Magic Square Technique was used as a spread spectrum technique to resize the watermark image.

3.2.1   Digital Watermark Embedding Procedure

The steps involved in embedding resized watermark into cover image based on the given architecture shown in Fig. 3.1 are as follows:

Step 1: Apply Magic Square procedure explained in Sect. 3.3.1 to obtain a resized image, RI and adjustment array, AD.

Step 2: Add The RI obtained through the magic square procedure is added in to third dimension or blue space of CI using Eq. 3.1.

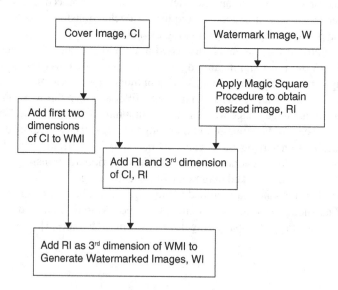

Fig. 3.1 MST-digital watermark embedding procedure

Fig. 3.2 MST-digital
watermark extraction
procedure

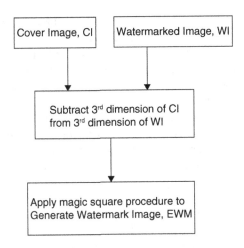

$$WMI_{m,n,3} = CI_{m,n,3} + RI_{m,n} \qquad (3.1)$$

Step 3: The red and green planes are added to WMI to produce a watermarked
image.

3.2.2   Digital Watermark Extraction Procedure

The steps involved in extracting watermark from the watermarked image based on
the given architecture shown in Fig. 3.2 are as follows:

Step 1: The 3-dimension values of CI are subtracted from the third dimension values
of WMI to obtain MSR, as per Eq. 3.2.

$$MSR_{m,n} = WMI_{m,n,3} - CI_{m,n,3} \qquad (3.2)$$

Step 2: The magic square application discussed in Sect. 3.3.1 is applied to extract
the watermark, EWM.
Step 3: The extracted watermark, EWM, is compared with the watermark, W

3.2.3   Experimental Results

A Lenna color image (Fig. 2.4a) of size 512×512 pixels was considered as a
cover image, CI. The block size was considered as 8×8 pixels. An array, MW, of
a size equivalent to the size of cover image was created with all zero values

initially and divided in to 64 equal blocks. A gray scale image with 64×64 pixels size was considered as watermark, W (Fig. 2.4b). The magic Square application discussed in Sect. 3.3.1 was applied on each pixel of W to generate a magic square for the given pixel value. The 64 elements of the obtained magic square are inserted into all blocks of MW at the respective pixel location as considered from W. This results in resized watermark consisting of 64 blocks of the given watermark with varying intensities and the image is as shown in Fig. 2.25. Figure 2.25 is multiplied by a factor of 10 for visual representation as shown in Fig. 2.26. The minimum value is 34 for which a 4×4 magic square can be generated. As per the magic square procedure discussed in Sect. 3.3.1, step 2, for all pixels of W an adjustment array, AD, was generated [5].

One quadrant of obtaining watermark was embedded to the blue component of cover image as discussed in Sect. 3.2.1. The obtained watermarked image is as shown in Fig. 3.3. The watermark is extracted from Fig. 3.3 based on the procedure discussed in Sect. 3.2.2 and is shown in Fig. 3.4.

The embedding and extraction procedures are applied on various 24-bit standard color images and watermarked images are obtained. These watermarked images are compared with respective original images and the results are tabulated in Table 3.1. The results demonstrate that the method discussed is better than the method given by Yuancheng Li [4] but generates noisy watermarked image.

The Lenna watermarked image (BMP image file) shown in Fig. 3.3 was compressed with GIF, JPEG, and PNG compression techniques, and the resulting watermarked images are shown in Figs. 3.5, 3.7, and 3.9, respectively. Similarly the watermark is extracted from these compressed images as discussed in the procedure Sect. 3.2.2, and the results are shown in Figs. 3.6, 3.8, and 3.10, respectively.

Fig. 3.3 Watermarked
Lenna BMP image (MST)

Fig. 3.4 Extracted
watermark from Fig. 3.3
(MST)

Table 3.1 PSNR results for various cover images (MST)

S. No.	Image name (size 512×512)	MST	Huang Hui-fen [7]	Yuancheng Li [4]	Patrizio Campisi et al. [3]
1	Lenna	33.04	39.9	27.7	40.46
2	Baboon	33.04	–	–	37.6
3	Barbara	33.05	–	–	40.14
4	Pepper	33.04	–	–	–

Fig. 3.5 Watermarked
Lenna image compressed
by GIF format (MST)

Fig. 3.6 Extracted
watermark from Fig. 3.5
(MST)

Fig. 3.7 Watermarked
Lenna image compressed
by JPEG format (MST)

Fig. 3.8 Extracted
watermark from Fig. 3.7
(MST)

Fig. 3.9 Watermarked
Lenna image compressed
by PNG format (MST)

Fig. 3.10 Extracted
watermark from Fig. 3.9
(MST)

The technique is tested for its performance by comparing the extracted water-mark with the original watermark (Fig. 2.4b), and the PSNR results are tabulated in Table 3.2. The results obtained show that the watermarks are noisy. So there is a need to strengthen the technique [5].

Table 3.2 Variation of PSNR for different compression formats (MST)

S. No.	Type of attack on 24-bit color Lenna image (Size 512×512)	PSNR obtained MST
1	Watermark extracted from BMP image	41.27
2	Bmp converted to GIF format	14.59
3	Bmp converted to JPEG format	14.49
4	Bmp converted to PNG format	14.57

3.3 Image Watermarking Based on the Magic Square and Ridgelet Transform (MSRTT)

Figure 3.11 explains the procedure for application of transforming technique on watermark and then embedding it into ridgelet transformed cover image to obtain watermarked image. Figure 3.12 explains the procedure for extraction of the watermark from the watermarked image by applying ridgelet transform technique. The extracted watermark will then be compared to the existing original watermark [6].

Fig. 3.11 MSRTT-digital watermark embedding procedure

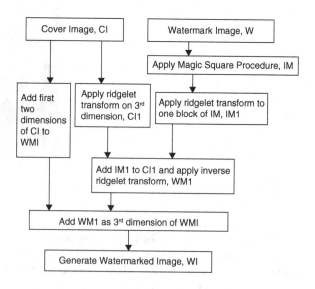

Fig. 3.12 MSRTT-digital
watermark extraction
procedure

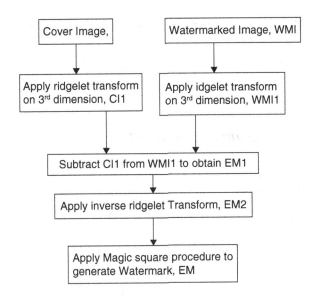

3.3.1   Digital Watermark Embedding Procedure

The steps involved in embedding ridgelets of resized watermark into the ridgelets of cover image based on the given architecture shown in Fig. 3.11 are as follows:

Step 1: The *ridgelet* function is applied on the third dimension of CI to obtain an array B.

Step 2: The watermark, W, is resized by using the magic square procedure discussed in 3.4.1 to obtain RI.

Step 3: one quadrant of RI is transformed by the ridgelet transform technique to obtain an array, C.

Step 4: The other pixel values of RI are stored as EM.

Step 5: The angle coefficients of B and C arrays are added as per Eqs. 3.3 and 3.4 to obtain an array RTP.

$$RTP_{\{m,1\}\{1,2\}\{1,k\}} \ = \ B_{\{m,1\}\{1,2\}\{1,k\}} \ + \ C_{\{m,1\}\{1,2\}\{1,k\}} \tag{3.3}$$

$$RTP_{\{m,1\}\{1,1\}\{1,k\}} \ = \ B_{\{m,1\}\{1,1\}\{1,k\}} \tag{3.4}$$

Step 6: The inverse ridgelet transform technique is applied to RTP to obtain third dimension of WMI.

Step 7: First two dimensions of CI are added to WI to obtain a watermarked image, WMI.

Step 8: The values of D obtained through Eq. 3.5 and B are stored for extraction purpose.

$$D_{\{m,1\}\{1,1\}\{1,k\}} \quad = \quad C_{\{m,1\}\{1,1\}\{1,k\}} \tag{3.5}$$

3.3.2 Digital Watermark Extraction Procedure

The steps involved in extracting watermark from ridgelets of watermarked image based on the given architecture shown in Fig. 3.12 are as follows:

Step 1: The ridgelet procedure is applied on third dimension of the array, WMI to obtain an array WMB.

Step 2: The ridgelet coefficients of B are subtracted from WMB to obtain the cells, D as per Eq. 3.6.

$$D_{\{m,1\}\{1,2\}\{1,k\}} \quad = \quad WMB_{\{m,1\}\{1,2\}\{1,k\}} \quad - \quad B_{\{m,1\}\{1,2\}\{1,k\}} \tag{3.6}$$

Step 3: The displacement values from array C are added to D and then inverse ridgelet transform technique is applied to obtain extracted watermark array, ExWM, as given in Eq. 3.7.

$$\text{ExWM} = \text{inv ridgelet}\left(C + D\right) \tag{3.7}$$

Step 4: The size of the extracted watermark will be $q \times q$ pixels. These pixels will be inserted into ExWM, from which the original watermark, EWM can be extracted by using adjustment array, ADJ, as per Eq. 3.8 to prove the authenticity.

$$EWM_{m,n} = \sum_{m=0}^{m} \sum_{n=0}^{m} \sum_{q=n+64}^{p} \left(ExWM_{m,q} + ADJ_{m,n} \right) \tag{3.8}$$

3.3.3 Experimental Results

A Lenna color image (Fig. 2.4a) of size 512×512 pixels is considered as a cover image, CI. The block size is considered as 8×8 pixels. An array, MW, of a size equivalent to the size of cover image is created with all zero values initially and divided into 64 equal blocks. A grayscale image with 64×64 pixels size is considered as watermark, W (Fig. 2.4b). The magic square application discussed in Sect. 2.3.1.2 is applied to each pixel of W to generate a magic square for the given pixel value. The 64 elements of the obtained magic square are inserted into all blocks of MW at the respective pixel location as considered from W. This results in resized watermark consisting of 64 blocks of the given watermark with varying intensities and the image are as shown in Fig. 2.25. Figure 2.26 is the complement image of Fig. 2.25. The minimum value is 34 for which a 4×4 magic square can be generated. As per the magic square procedure discussed in Sect. 2.3.1.2, for all pixels of W an adjustment array, AD, is generated [5].

The *ridgelet* function is applied on the third dimension of cover image (CI) to obtain an array B consisting of 1024 cells (The number of possible center slices present in B is $512 + 512 = 1024$). Each output in the cells corresponds to ridgelet transform coefficient at a particular angle. The 128×128 pixel block of resized watermark array RI obtained from the magic square procedure is taken and the ridgelet transform technique is applied to obtain an array, C. The ridgelet coefficients of B and C arrays are added and the inverse ridgelet transform technique is applied to obtain the watermarked image, WMI (as shown in Fig. 3.16). The watermark is extracted from the watermarked image (shown in Fig. 3.13), and 64×64 pixel watermark is reconstructed as per the given procedure (shown in Fig. 3.14). The obtained watermark is

Fig. 3.13 Watermarked Lenna BMP image (MSRTT)

Fig. 3.14 Extracted watermark from Fig. 3.13 (MSRTT)

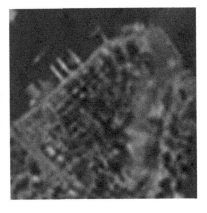

compared with the original watermark (Fig. 2.4b). The resultant PSNR has shown an acceptable level of noise in the watermarked image [6].

The embedding and extraction procedures are applied on various 24-bit standard color images, and watermarked images are obtained. These watermarked images are compared with respective original images and the results are tabulated in Table 3.3. The results demonstrate that the method discussed is better than all the other methods discussed by Huang Hui-fen [7], Yuancheng Li [4], and Patrizio Campisi et al. [3].

The Lenna watermarked image (BMP image file) shown in Fig. 3.13 is compressed with GIF, JPEG, and PNG compression techniques, and the resulting watermarked images are shown in Figs. 3.15, 3.17, and 3.19, respectively. Similarly the watermark is extracted from these compressed images as discussed in the procedure Sect. 3.3.2, and the results are shown in Figs. 3.16, 3.18, and 3.20, respectively.

The technique is tested for its performance by comparing the extracted watermark with the original watermark (Fig. 2.4b), and the PSNR results are tabulated in Table 3.4. The resultant PSNR shows that the obtained watermarks are noisy. It is also observed that the GIF compression technique affects more the watermark information embedded into watermarked image.

Table 3.3 PSNR results for various cover images (MSRTT)

S. No.	Image name (size 512×512)	MSRTT	Huang Hui-fen [7]	Yuancheng Li [4]	Patrizio Campisi et al. [3]
1	Lenna	61.93	39.9	27.7	40.46
2	Baboon	61.93	–	–	37.6
3	Barbara	61.93	–	–	40.14
4	Pepper	62.03	–	–	–

Fig. 3.15 Watermarked Lenna image compressed by GIF format (MSRTT)

Fig. 3.16 Extracted watermark from Fig. 3.15 (MSRTT)

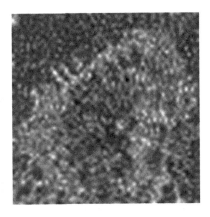

Fig. 3.17 Watermarked Lenna image compressed by JPEG format (MSRTT)

Fig. 3.18 Extracted watermark from Fig. 3.17 (MSRTT)

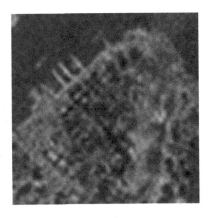

Fig. 3.19 Watermarked
Lenna image compressed
by PNG format (MSRTT)

Fig. 3.20 Extracted
watermark from Fig. 3.19
(MSRTT)

Table 3.4 Variation of PSNR for different compression formats (MSRTT)

S. No.	Type of attack on 24-bit color Lenna image (Size 512×512)	PSNR obtained MSRTT
1	Watermark extracted from BMP image	38.63
2	Bmp converted to GIF format	15.02
3	Bmp converted to JPEG format	25.84
4	Bmp converted to PNG format	38.63

3.4 Summary

This chapter presents a brief review of the abovementioned methods and then their performance evaluation by comparing with each other and also with other published works. Table 3.5 gives the PSNR of the various watermarked images comparison with the respective cover images. The results demonstrate that the MSRTT outperforms all other techniques [6].

Table 3.6 provides a comparative study of the extracted watermarks obtained by the methods discussed in this chapter. The results demonstrated that the watermark extracted from the watermarked image in MSRTT possessed its characteristics even after undergoing various compression attacks.

Table 3.5 PSNR results for various cover images—Ridgelet techniques

S. No.	Image name (size 512×512)	MST	MSRTT	Huang Hui-fen [7]	Yuancheng Li [4]	Patrizio Campisi et al. [3]
1	Lenna	33.04	61.93	39.9	27.7	40.46
2	Baboon	33.04	61.93	–	–	37.6
3	Barbara	33.05	61.93	–	–	40.14
4	Pepper	33.04	62.03	–	–	–

Table 3.6 Variation of PSNR for different compression formats—Ridgelet techniques

S. No.	Type of attack on 24-bit color Lenna image (Size 512×512)	PSNR obtained	
		MST	MSRTT
1	Watermark extracted from BMP image	41.27	38.63
2	Bmp converted to GIF format	14.59	15.02
3	Bmp converted to JPEG format	14.49	25.84
4	Bmp converted to PNG format	14.57	38.63

References

1. David L. Donoho & Ana Georgina Flesia, "Digital Ridgelet Transform based on True Ridge Functions", International Journal of Studies in Computational Mathematics, Vol. 10, 2003, pp. 1–30
2. Jean-Luc Starck, Emmanuel J. Candès & David L. Donoho, "The Curvelet Transform for Image Denoising", IEEE Transactions on Image Processing, Vol. 11, No. 6, 2002, pp. 670-684
3. Patrizio Campisi, Deepa Kundur & Alessandro Neri, "Robust Digital Watermarking in the Ridgelet Domain", IEEE Signal Processing Letters, Vol. 11, No. 10, 2004, pp. 826-830

4. Yuancheng Li, "An Image Digital Watermarking Method Based On Ridgelet and KICA", International Conference on MultiMedia and Information Technology (MMIT), 2008, pp. 345-348
5. Channapragada R. S. R. & Munaga V. N. K. Prasad, "Digital Watermarking Based on Magic Square and Ridgelet Transform Techniques", Intelligent Computing, Networking, and Informatics (International Conference on Advanced Computing, Networking and Informatics-Advances in Intelligent Systems and Computing), Vol. 243, 2014, pp. 143-161.
6. Minh N. Do & Martin Vetterli, "The Finite Ridgelet Transform for Image Representation", IEEE Transactions on Image Processing, Vol. 12, Issue. 1, 2003, pp. 16–28
7. Huang Hui-fen, "Perceptual Image Watermarking Algorithm Based on Magic Squares Scrambling in DWT", 5th International Joint conference on INC, IMS, IDC, 2009, pp. 1819-1822

Chapter 4
Digital Watermarking Using Fractals

Abstract Two techniques, namely digital image watermarking using fractals (DWF)) and digital image watermarking based on fractals and curvelets (DWFC), are discussed in this chapter. In DWF, the host image is encoded by the proposed fractal coding method. To embed the watermark evenly over the whole host image, specific range blocks are selected. Then, the scrambled watermark is inserted into the selected range blocks. Finally, the watermarked image is obtained by the fractal decoding method. In DWFC, the technique implements curvelet transform on the original color image to obtain curvelet coefficients. These coefficients are then transformed by using 2-level DWT to get LL2 and LL1 low-frequency sub-bands. The mutual similarities between LL1 and LL2 sub-bands are considered for embedding watermark. The obtained watermarked image has better quality when compared to a few exiting methods. The results indicate that the embedding procedures of DWF and DWFC are superior to MSRTT, and extraction procedures of DWF and DWFC are comparable to MSRTT. The regeneration of watermark image is satisfactory.

4.1 Introduction

This chapter deals with the design and development of the digital watermark technique based on fractals and curvelet transform procedures for color images. The chapter briefly discusses the prerequisite fractal techniques for understanding the proposed digital watermarking technique.

Many researchers have presented robust, fragile, and semi-fragile watermarking solutions [19–21]. Li and Wang [18] have presented a technique for embedding the watermark by using fractal image coding. Puate and Jordan [24] have presented a technique in which the fractal technique is applied to compress the cover image and then the watermark embedded. Barni et al. [14] have applied discrete cosine transform technique on the cover image, then the watermark is embedded. Jian Ping Huang [22] has discussed digital watermarking technique based on finite ridgelet transform (FRIT) technique. The smallest segments of the watermark are transformed using FRIT and then a sparse matrix is generated based on selected

© The Author(s) 2016
C.R.S. Rao, M.V.N.K. Prasad, *Digital Watermarking Techniques in Curvelet and Ridgelet Domain*, SpringerBriefs in Computer Science, DOI 10.1007/978-3-319-32951-2_4

points, which is considered for embedding. The embedding and extraction procedures have proven the technique's robustness against tamper orientation. Jayamohan and Revathy [23] have presented a method using fractal theory and DWT. In this the original image is segmented into small blocks to calculate the local fractal dimension of each block by using differential box counting (DBC). The watermarked image is obtained by embedding the DWT coefficients of watermark into fractals. Bhatnagar et al. [17] have presented a method based on factional packet wavelet transform technique. The cover image is segmented into small chunks and is transformed based on fractional packet wavelet transform procedure. The resultant image and the watermark are segmented and SVD transformed and embedded. The inverse SVD procedure results with the watermarked image which has proven its robustness against tampering.

Fatemeh Daraee and Saeed Mozaffari [25] have presented a technique for coding the host image by the fractal coding technique. The watermark is embedded to the number of ones in the selected range segments which are selected through the predefined conditions to obtain the watermarked Image. Rao and Prasad [11] have presented two techniques based on magic square and ridgelet transform techniques. The methods spread the watermark to a renewed size by using the magic square technique and then embed it into the ridgelets of the host image. Rao and Prasad [12] have presented four different techniques based on magic square and curvelet transform techniques. In two methods the curvelets of watermark are added to curvelets of the original image. In the other two techniques the watermark is resized by using a magic square technique and then embedded into the curvelets of the host image. Satoshi Ohga and Ryuji Hamabe have presented a watermarking technique to embed the watermark in fractals of the original image. In this technique the wavelets of original image obtained and then by using fractal image coding the watermark are embedded in LL1. The human visual model presented by Barni et al. [16] was used to improve the watermarked image. It is observed that there is a need to improve the technique without HVS model, which has motivated to propose a technique making the modifications for improving the results.

4.2   Digital Image Watermarking Using Fractals

In this watermarking technique, at first Lenna color image (I) of size $M \times N$ is taken and divided into RGB components. From this Blue component of the image as shown in Fig. 4.1a is considered for embedding watermark as it is less prone towards noise attacks [26]. Next, this blue component undergoes bit plane slicing in which 8 bit planes are formed since each pixel contains only 8 bits. In this method fourth and fifth bit planes as shown in Fig. 4.1b, c respectively are used for fractal coding and watermark insertion. Fractals are irregular and fragmented shapes surrounding an image. The term fractal was coined by mathematician Benoit Mandelbrot in 1975 [7]. Mandelbrot derived it from the Latin word fractus, which means irregular, broken, or fractured. The two main properties of fractals are self-similarity and self-reference [7].

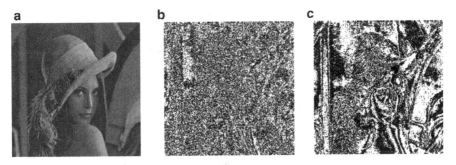

Fig. 4.1 (**a**) Blue component of Lenna color image, (**b**) 4-bit plane of blue component, (**c**) 5-bit plane of blue component

4.2.1 Digital Watermark Embedding Procedure

The procedure consists of four major steps: fractal encoding of host image, scrambling the watermark, embedding into the fractal code, and fractal decoding to obtain the watermarked image [8].

Step 1. Fractal block coding involves selecting a suitable range and domain block pairs and manipulating various parameters like luminous offset (g) contrast scaling (s). The process of converting fractal code from the given image is called fractal encoding or fractal image compression. In this method, range blocks are taken from the fourth bit plane and the domain block pool is from the fifth bit plane. Both the range and domain blocks are of equal sizes, i.e., b×b. The numbers of range and domain blocks obtained are M/b×N/b. Next, for each range block (Rb), a block is searched in the domain block pool (Db) which is most similar to the range block. Here, the similarity of the range and domain blocks is calculated using the correlation. If the correlation is more, similarity is more. From this, the best range–domain block pair is found and the range block is modified as per Eq. 4.1.

$$R = s \times \arg\max\left(corr2\left(Rb, Db\right)\right) + g \times U) \tag{4.1}$$

Where s stands for contrast scaling, g stands for luminous offset, and U stands for unit matrix. For each range block of the image, the fractal code is calculated using Eq. 4.1 and stored as {Rb, R}, where Rb is an original range block and R is the modified Range block (Fig. 4.2) [8].

Step 2. Watermark (Wm) of size wm×wn is shuffled first as shown in Fig. 4.3b before being embedded into fourth × bit plane of blue component of color image. The shuffling process is employed by the scrambling with a seed K, where K

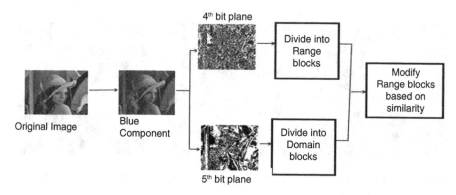

Fig. 4.2 Fractal encoding procedure for color host image

plays the role of secret key. Therefore, K secretly belongs to the legal owner. Scramble (K, Wm) generates a random number of sequences of permutation positions for all bits of Wm with each bit w(p, q) (where p, q represent position). Wm is rearranged into another position, so that the rearranged Wm is Wm′ = { w′(p, q) | 0≤p, q≤64, w′(p, q)=0 or 1}. Because of this, the watermarked image becomes more robust when it undergoes a cropping attack.

Step 3. For watermark embedding consider fourth bit plane, which was undergone fractal compression and all range blocks of this bit plane were modified and represented as R where size of each range block is b×b and number of range blocks are M/b × M/b. Divide R into m×n sets called S such that wm=m, wn=n and each set contains 2×2 Range blocks. Wmv is embedded into S, which is of the same size. For every set of 4 range blocks of R one bit of watermark are embedded. Find the blocks B_{max} and B_{min} for every set, where B_{max} and B_{min} represent the blocks having maximum and minimum number of 1's present respectively. Block (WB) is selected from a set of 4 blocks and watermark bit is inserted into the first pixel using XOR operator. This WB block is determined based on watermark to be inserted into that block, i.e., if,

$$w'(p,q) = \begin{cases} 0, WB = B_{min} \text{ of } S(p,q) \\ 1, WB = B_{max} \text{ of } S(p,q) \end{cases} \qquad (4.2)$$

Select WB block for each watermark bit of Wmv. The indexes of WB are stored as a secret key which is used during watermark extraction process. Then the watermarked block is formed using Eq. 4.3 by changing the original block. Remaining blocks of set are not modified, and fractal decoding is used for watermarked image construction. This will result in the watermarked image as shown in Fig. 4.4.

$$WB(1,1) = w'(p,q) XOR WB(1,1) \qquad (4.3)$$

Fig. 4.3 (**a**) Original watermark image, (**b**) scrambled watermark image

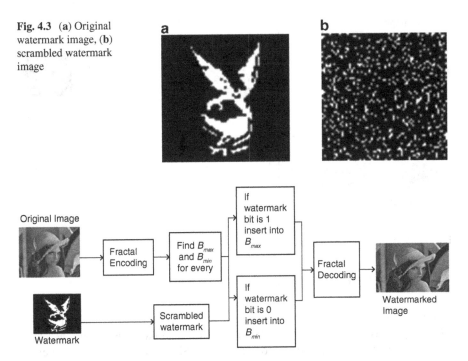

Fig. 4.4 Watermark embedding procedure

Step 4. The process of image reconstruction from fractal codes is called fractal decoding. Decoding of original images from fractal codes is an iterative process of reconstruction of range blocks from the set of fractal code parameters. Since it is a binary image decoding, it takes one iteration only. After getting the watermarked range blocks, the image is constructed using these blocks. Four bit plane of watermarked image is constructed using fractal decoding techniques. Then combine this bit plane with the remaining 7 bit planes of original blue components of the color image. This watermarked blue component is again combined with red and green components of the original color image. Thus, the watermarked color image (WI) is formed.

4.2.2   Digital Watermark Extraction Procedure

To extract the watermark image, both watermarked image and the host image are needed. First, range blocks of both host and watermarked images are calculated. Fractal codes are calculated from host image using the proposed method shown in Fig. 4.5. Using the indexes that stored in secret key range blocks having watermark bit are found and watermark bits are extracted by applying the XOR operator between the range blocks of the host image and watermarked image. Using the seed K that stored in secret key descrambling is done and the watermark image is produced.

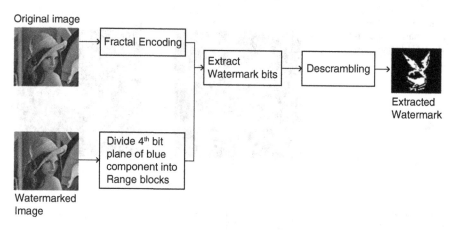

Fig. 4.5 Watermark extraction procedure

4.2.3   Experimental Results

In this section, the performance evaluation of digital image watermarking algorithms is discussed. The quality of the proposed fractal based watermarking technique i evaluated using peak signal to noise ratio (PSNR) and correlation coefficient as discussed in Sect 1.8.

The correlation coefficient is a number representing the similarity between two images in relation with their respective pixel intensity. The correlation coefficient between A and B is calculated as per given Eq. 4.4.

$$r = \frac{\sum_m \sum_n \left(A_{mn} - A\right)\left(B_{mn} - \bar{B}\right)}{\sqrt{\left(\sum_m \sum_n \left(A_{mn} - A\right)^2\right)\left(\sum_m \sum_n \left(B_{mn} - \bar{B}\right)^2\right)}} \tag{4.4}$$

Where $\bar{A}$ = mean^2 (A), $\bar{B}$ = mean^2 (B). All experiments are conducted on standard color images with the size of 512×512 like Lenna, Baboon, Barbara, Pepper. Watermark image is a binary image of size 64×64. Range and domain blocks have the size of 4×4. Figure 4.6 shows the watermarked image and the extracted watermark image after applying the proposed procedure.

Table 4.1 gives the PSNR and correlation results when the original image is compared with the obtained watermarked image. The table also demonstrates various results based on varied range block size. The results show that the correlation between the obtained watermarked image and the original image is the highest value. Even though the payload increases, PSNR increases because the range block size decreases, i.e., the most similar block which has been found during fractal encoding will be almost equal. Table 4.2 gives the comparative study of the proposed method with other methods discussed by Jian Lu et al. [1] and Soheila Kiani et al. [2].

Fig. 4.6 (**a**) Watermarked
Lenna image
(PSNR = 51.6582 dB) (**b**)
extracted watermark with
correlation coefficient = 1.0

a

b
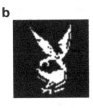

Table 4.1 PSNR of the watermarked image and correlation coefficient of the extracted watermark for different host images

Host image	Range block size	Size of watermark (bits)	PSNR of watermarked image	Extracted watermark correlation coefficient
Lenna	2×2	128×128	56.4008	1.0
	4×4	64×64	51.6582	1.0
	8×8	32×32	48.2552	1.0
Barbara	2×2	128×128	56.9801	1.0
	4×4	64×64	51.9967	1.0
	8×8	32×32	48.6438	1.0
Baboon	2×2	128×128	56.6184	1.0
	4×4	64×64	52.0403	1.0
	8×8	32×32	49.1262	1.0
Pepper	2×2	128×128	56.6184	1.0
	4×4	64×64	51.6822	1.0
	8×8	32×32	48.2985	1.0

Table 4.2 PSNR Results for various cover images (DWF)

Methods	Payload (bits)	Lenna (dB)	Baboon (dB)	Barbara (dB)	Pepper (dB)
Jian Lu et al. [1]	128×128	34.71		30.37	32.01
Soheila Kiani et al. [2]	512	49.86			47.65
Proposed method	64×64	51.6582	51.9967	52.0403	51.6822
	128×128	56.4008	56.6184	56.9801	56.3412
	512	51.9927	52.3482	52.6715	51.8213

Table 4.3 Correlation coefficient of original watermark and extracted watermark obtained after cropping attack, salt and pepper noise attack, and JPEG compression on watermarked image

Attacks	Lenna	Baboon	Barbara	Pepper
Cropping				
Type-1	0.7210	0.7292	0.7488	0.7555
Type-2	0.6848	0.7043	0.6980	0.7260
Type-3	0.4906	0.4860	0.4880	0.5188
Salt and pepper				
Type-1	0.9784	0.9840	0.9720	0.9804
Type-2	0.9188	0.9098	0.9054	0.9075
Type-3	0.8507	0.8330	0.8720	0.8362
JPEG compression	0.9880	0.9853	0.9807	0.9895
TIF compression	1	1	1	1

The watermarked image's robustness is evaluated by attacking the image through various image manipulation procedures like cropping, adding noise and compression. Then the watermark is extracted from these manipulated images and compared with the original watermark image. Table 4.3 gives the correlation results when the original watermark is compared with extracted watermark from various attacked watermarked images.

4.3 Digital Image Watermarking Based on Fractals and Curvelets

This section discusses an image watermarking technique based on fractal theory, curvelet transformation and DWT. Fractal image coding is based on iterated function system (IFS). The IFS is based on the idea of self similarity possession by the natural images [15] which is used to code the image in fractal image coding. The cover image is segmented into low and high frequency sub-bands by using DWT [20, 27].

4.3.1 Digital Watermark Embedding Procedure

The original image is transformed through the curvelet transform technique [13], i.e., the original image is transformed using 2D Fast Fourier transformation (FFT) technique. Then for each scale–angle pair, calculate the sample values inside the parallelepiped. Multiply the interpolated object with the parabolic window which effectively localizes near the parallelepiped with orientation and apply an inverse FFT to obtain curvelet transform coefficients, CT, of the given image. The transformed coefficients are then transformed using 2 level DWT to obtain LL2 and LL1 sub-bands. LL1 is segmented into nonoverlapping range blocks, R, of size $m \times m$.

LL2 is segmented into overlapping domain blocks, D, of same size as range blocks, i.e., $m \times m$ with a sliding step size, δ [9]. The even and odd blocks of the domain blocks are separated based on Eq. 4.5.

$$D_{i,j} \in \begin{cases} C_0 & \text{if } (i+j) \bmod 2 = 0 \\ C_1 & \text{if } (i+j) \bmod 2 \neq 0 \end{cases} \tag{4.5}$$

where i and j are index values, C0 and C1 are domain classes, and D are domain blocks. The domain blocks, D, are transformed through a number of suitable affine transformations like identity transformation, reflection about a vertical axis, reflection about a horizontal axis, reflection about main diagonal, reflection about anti-diagonal, rotation about center of the block (90° or 180° or 270°). A candidate range block, R, is compared with transformed domain blocks and a suitable match is considered where the mean square error between R and D can be neglected. The watermark bit is then added into the domain block and is then placed in LL1 sub-band and the index information on the D is stored for extraction purpose as key. The inverse 2 level DWT is obtained and then the inverse curvelet procedure applied to obtain the watermarked image. The watermark can be embedded a number of times (U), and if the U increases, the quality of watermarked image decreases.

4.3.2   Digital Watermark Extraction Procedure

The watermarked image is first transformed by using curvelet transform technique and then 2 level DWT is applied to obtain LL1 and LL2 sub-bands. The $m \times m$ number of nonoverlapping range blocks are constructed by using LL1 sub-band. The $m \times m$ number of overlapping domain blocks with sliding step δ are constructed by using LL2 sub-band. The odd and even domain blocks are obtained through Eq. 4.5. The stored key information is applied to select an appropriate range block, R, and then the watermark bit embedded in that block is extracted by using Eq. 4.6.

$$W_b' = \begin{cases} 0 & \text{if } (i+j) \bmod 2 = 0 \\ 1 & \text{if } (i+j) \bmod 2 \neq 0 \end{cases} \tag{4.6}$$

Where i, j, b are index values and W is watermark. The above procedure is repeated for extracting all watermark bits by using all the stored key values.

4.3.3   Experimental Results

This section presents the results obtained by implementing the procedures discussed in the previous section on standard color images of size 512×512 pixels to embed 32 bits binary sequence watermark. The cover image, I, of size 512×512 is transformed by using curvelet transform technique to obtain a transformed image, CT. CT is transformed by applying 2-level DWT to obtain LL1 and LL2. LL1 is partitioned into nonoverlapping small blocks of size 4×4 known as range blocks, R. LL2 is partitioned into overlapping small blocks of size 4×4 with sliding step size $\delta = 1$, known as domain blocks, D. The domain blocks are portioned into two classes called C0 and C1 based on Eq. 4.5. The range blocks are sorted in descending order with respect to the block variance value. Based on the watermark bit the domain block, D, belonging to C0 or C1 is selected. The block D is transformed by affine transformation and then compared with range blocks. A range block, Ri, is selected whose mean square error with that of the transformed domain block D is negligible. The domain block D is modified with the watermark bit and the information is stored as key. The process is repeated for all watermark bits. Then the inverse transformation is applied to obtain the watermarked image.

Generally, if there is an alteration in low frequency sub-bands, the change is reflected by degradation in image quality, which is minimal in the above procedure due to the watermark embedded in the edges. Little degradation is compensated while taking inverse curvelet transform. Also the degradation is low if the watermark size is small and is embedded only a limited number of times. The redundancy factor is less, when the watermark is embedded in LL1 for 3–4 times at maximum rather than embedding the watermark 10 times in high frequency sub-bands which takes most of toll in case of an attack. For smaller values of redundancy (U = 1) the PSNR is as high as 53.42 dB and for U = 5 the PSNR is 53.26 dB and for U = 10 the PSNR is found to be 44.96 dB for Lenna color image. Figures 4.7, 4.8, and 4.9 show watermarked images for different redundancy factor U for Lenna.

Fig. 4.7 Watermarked image for redundancy factor U = 1 (PSNR = 53.42 dB)

Fig. 4.8 Watermarked
image for redundancy
factor U = 5
(PSNR = 46.54 dB)

Fig. 4.9 Watermarked
image for redundancy
factor U = 10
(PSNR = 44.96 dB)

Table 4.4 gives the comparison between original and watermarked images for different images like Lenna, Baboon, Barbara and Pepper when U = 1. The results are comparable with the results obtained through various methods presented in refs. [3–6, 10, 22]. The method by Satoshi Ohga and Ryuji Hamabe uses 256×256 pixel size gray scale original Lenna image for embedding 32-bit watermark through without and with HVS model applied techniques [10]. The technique discussed by Jian Ping Huang uses 512×512 pixel grayscale Lenna image and is embedded with its transformed image [22]. The technique discussed by Yan Li et al. embeds a 48×48 pixel watermark into 512×512 pixel grayscale Lenna image [3]. Nima

Table 4.4 PSNR Results for various cover images (DWFC)

S. No.	BMP image name (size 512×512)	Proposed method U = 1	Calculated PSNR in dB						
			Satoshi Ohga. and Ryuji Hamabe [10]		Jian Ping Huang., 2008 [22]	Yan Li, Shengqian Wang and Zhihua Xie [3]	Nima Khademi Kalantari and Seyed Mohammad Ahadi [5]	Hai Yan Yu and Xiao Li Zhang [6]
			With HVS	Without HVS				
1	Lenna	53.42	38.72	41.32	38.62	42.45	45	40.72
2	Baboon	49.96					45	
3	Barbara	53.97						
4	Pepper	51.89						

Table 4.5 Variation of PSNR for different compression formats (DWFC)

S. No.	Type of attack on 24 bit color Lenna image	*PSNR obtained*
1	Watermark extracted from BMP image	Inf
2	Bmp converted to GIF format	54.15
3	Bmp converted to JPEG format	56.19
4	Bmp converted to PNG format	Inf

Khademi Kalantari and Seyed Mohammad Ahadi discussed a method in which 256 bits of watermark are embedded into 510×510 grayscale original image [5]. Hai Yan Yu and Xiao Li Zhang have embedded a watermark sequence into 510×510 pixel grayscale original images [6]. Table 4.5 gives the PSNR results after attacks on Lenna watermarked image.

It is observed that depending on the curvelet transform of the image under consideration, the data hiding capacity and image quality vary. But in general, the watermark can be embedded in any image up to 10 times without visual degradation. Human eye cannot perceive the degradation very easily if the PSNR is more than 40 dB.

4.4 Summary

In this chapter, we describe methods based on fractal color image watermarking that have been developed and assessed for their performance. The main objectives of watermarking are imperceptibility and to achieve robustness against attacks. The results of the first technique show that the method is comparable to the methods discussed by Jian Lu et al. [1] and Soheila Kiani et al. [2]. In the second technique, the robustness performance is very high for watermark embedding method. However, the redundancy degree, i.e., the number of times the watermark embedded, is a complex problem as the redundancy increases the noise in watermarked image increases. Through this method we have overcome this problem as the watermark gets embedded into the significant curvatures of the image. It is compensated by stronger robustness performance against image compression attacks.

References

1. Jian Lu, Yuru Zou, Chaoying Yang, and Lijing Wang, "A Robust Fractal Color Image Watermarking Algorithm", Mathematical Problems in Engineering, Volume 3, 2014, pp. 1-12.
2. Soheila Kiani, Mohsen Ebrahimi Moghaddam, "A multi-purpose digital image watermarking using fractal block coding", The Journal of Systems and Software 84, 2011, pp. 1550-1562.
3. Yan Li, Shengqian Wang and Zhihua Xie, "A Local Watermarking Scheme in the Ridgelet Domain Combining Image Content and JND Model", International Conference on Computational Intelligence and Security, 2008, pp. 336–341.

4. P. Mangaiyarkarasi and S. Arulselvi, "A new Digital Image Watermarking based on Finite Ridgelet Transform and Extraction using ICA", International Conference on Emerging Trends in Electrical and Computer Technology, 2011, pp. 837-841.
5. Nima Khademi Kalantari and Seyed Mohammad Ahadi, "A Robust Image Watermarking in the Ridgelet Domain Using Universally Optimum Decoder", IEEE Transactions on Circuits and Systems for Video Technology, Vol. 20, No. 3, 2010, pp. 396-406
6. Hai Yan Yu and Xiao Li Zhang, "A Robust Watermark Algorithm Based on Ridgelet Transform and Fuzzy C-Means", International Symposium on Information Engineering and Electronic Commerce, 2009, 120-124.
7. Hsien-Chu Wu, Chin-Chen Chang, "Hiding Digital Watermarks Using Fractal Compression Technique", Fundamental informatica, Vol. 58, 2003, pp. 189-202.
8. Rama Seshagiri Rao Channapragada, & Munaga V.N.K. Prasad, "Digital Watermarking Using Fractal Coding", second International Symposium on Signal Processing and Intelligent Recognition Systems, 2015, pp. 109-118.
9. Rama Seshagiri Rao Channapragada & Munaga. V. N. K. Prasad, "Watermarking Using Ridgelets and fractal coding", Innovative Research in Attention Modeling and Computer Vision Applications, Eds. Rajarshi Pal, IGI Global Publications, pp. 388-399.
10. Satoshi Ohga and Ryuji Hamabe, (2014). "Digital Watermarking based on fractal image coding using DWT and HVS", International Journal of Knowledge-based and Intelligent Engineering Systems, Vol. 18, 81-89
11. Rama Seshagiri Rao Channapragada, Anil Srimanth Mantha & Munaga V.N.K. Prasad, (2012). "Study of Contemporary Digital watermarking Techniques", International Journal of Computer Science Issues, Vol. 9, Issue. 6, No. 1, pp. 456-464
12. Rama Seshagiri Rao Channapragada & Munaga V. N. K. Prasad,(2015). "Digital Watermarking Techniques in Curvelet Transformation Domain", Proceedings of the International Conference on CIDM, Vol. 1: Smart Innovation, Systems and Technologies, Volume 31, pp 199-211.
13. Minh N. Do & Martin Vetterli,(2003). "The Finite Ridgelet Transform for Image Representation", IEEE Transactions on Image Processing, Vol. 12, Issue. 1, pp. 16–28
14. M. Barni, F. Bartolini, V. Cappellini and A. Piva,(1998). "A DCT-domain system for robust image watermarking", Signal Processing, Vol. 66, No. 8, 357–371.
15. Arnaud E. Jacquin, (1992). "Image Coding Based on a Fractal Theory of Iterated Contractive Image Transformations", IEEE Transactions on Image Processing. Vol. 1 No. 1.
16. M. Barni, F. Bartolini and A. Piva,(2001). "Improved wavelet-based watermarking through pixel-wise masking", IEEE Transactions of Image Process, Vol. 10, No. 5, 783–791.
17. Bhatnagar, G., Raman, B. & Wu, Q.M.J.(2012). "Robust watermarking using fractional wavelet packet transform", IET Image Process., 6(4), 386–397.
18. C. Li and S. Wang, (2000). "Digital watermarking using fractal image coding", IEICE Trans on Fundamentals E83-A, Vol. 6, 1268-1288.
19. Channapragada R. S. G. Rao, V. Ravi, Munaga. V. N. K. Prasad & E. V. Gopal (2014). "Watermarking Using Artificial Intelligence Techniques", in "Encyclopedia of Business Analytics and Optimization", Eds. James W., IGI Global Publications Vol. 5, pp. 436-448
20. Channapragada R. S. G. Rao, V. Ravi, Munaga. V. N. K. Prasad & E. V. Gopal (2014). "Digital Watermarking Techniques for Images – Survey", "Encyclopedia of Business Analytics and Optimization", Eds. James W., IGI Global Publications, Vol. 2, pp. 191-200.
21. Channapragada R. S. G. Rao, V. Ravi, Munaga. V. N. K. Prasad & E. V. Gopal (2014). "Watermarking Using Intelligent Methods - Survey", in "Encyclopedia of Business Analytics and Optimization", Eds. James W., IGI Global Publications, Vol. 5, pp. 449-462.
22. Jian Ping Huang (2008). "A Fast Watermarking Algorithm for Image Authentication", International Conference on Cyberworlds, pp. 511-514
23. Jayamohan and Revathy (2012). "A Hybrid Fractal-Wavelet Digital Watermarking Technique with Localized Embedding Strength", 6th International Conference on Information Processing, 584-591.

24. J. Puate and F. Jordan, (1997). "Using fractal compression scheme to embed a digital signature into an image", SIPIE Photonics, Vol. 2915,108–118

25. Fatemeh Daraee and Saeed Mozaffari, (2014). "Watermarking in binary document images using fractal codes", Pattern Recognition Letters, Vol. 35, 120–129

26. I.J. Cox, M.L. Miller, J.A. Bloom, (2002). "Digital Watermarking", Academic Press, 2002.

27. H.J.M. Wang, P.C. Su and C.C.J. Kuo,(1998). "Wavelet-based digital image watermarking", Opt Express, Vol. 3, No. 12, 491–496.

Chapter 5
Conclusions and Future Scope

Eight different digital watermarking techniques are discussed in this book. These techniques have been tested for their performance against various image compression attacks. The outcome of the work done so far and the future direction of work is discussed in this chapter.

5.1 Conclusions and Limitations

The following points are observed.

- It is observed that the magic square technique spreads the brightness of the watermark to generate multiple copies of the given watermark as a resized image. However, it may degrade the quality of the same in some images.
- It is observed that in WCT and RWCT embedding of the watermark without transformation into the curvelets and ridgelets results greater noise levels in cover image.
- It is found the obtained PSNR values demonstrate that the curvelet transform technique is suitable for embedding transformed watermarks but the extraction process results in lossy watermark images.
- Similarly the PSNR results demonstrated that the ridgelet transform technique is more suitable and efficient in embedding process with satisfactory extraction process.
- It is observed that fractals technique is more suitable and efficient in embedding process and extraction process when the payload is binary digital content.

© The Author(s) 2016
C.R.S. Rao, M.V.N.K. Prasad, *Digital Watermarking Techniques in Curvelet and Ridgelet Domain*, SpringerBriefs in Computer Science,
DOI 10.1007/978-3-319-32951-2_5

5.2 Future Scope

- The performance of the digital watermarking methods designed, developed, and tested in this book are evaluated against compression attacks only, so this can be extended to other image processing attacks like cropping, scaling, and rotating.
- These techniques are not tested for video watermarking. So this can be considered as an extension of research as the video consists of a stream of frames and the hacker may delete the frame(s) consisting of authentication information without quality degradation.

Printed in the United States
By Bookmasters